Paul Simon's
Concert In The Park

Amsco Publications
New York/London/Sydney

MICHAEL BRECKER: *SAX/EWI*

MINGO ARAÚJO: *PERCUSSION*

The Obvious Child
Paul Simon

Well, I'm accustomed to a smooth ride,
Or maybe I'm a dog who's lost its bite.
I don't expect to be treated like a fool
    no more,
I don't expect to sleep through the night.
Some people say a lie's a lie's a lie,
But I say why,
Why deny the obvious child?
Why deny the obvious child?
And in remembering a road sign,
I am remembering a girl when I was young.
And we said, "These songs are true,
These days are ours,
These tears are free.
And hey,
The cross is in the ballpark,
The cross is in the ballpark."
We had a lot of fun,
We had a lot of money.
We had a little son and we thought
    we'd call him Sonny.
Sonny gets married and moves away,
Sonny has a baby and bills to pay.
Sonny gets sunnier
Day by day by day by day.
Doh doh, doh doh.
Doh doh, doh doh.

Well, I've been waking up at sunrise,
I've been following the light across
    my room.
I watch the night receive the room of
    my day.
Some people say the sky is just the sky,
But I say,
Why deny the obvious child?
Why deny the obvious child?
(Mm, mm, mm.)
Sonny sits by his window and he thinks
    to himself
How it's strange that some rooms are
    like cages.
Sonny's yearbook from high school
Is down from the shelf,
And he idly thumbs through the pages.
Some have died,
Some have fled from themselves,
Or struggled from here to get there.
Sonny wanders beyond his interior walls,
Runs his hand through his thinning
    brown hair.

Well, I'm accustomed to a smoother ride,
Or maybe I'm a dog who's lost its bite.
I don't expected to be treated like a fool
    no more,
I don't expect to sleep the night.
Some people say a lie is just a lie,
But I say, the cross is in the ball park.
Why deny the obvious child?

*Copyright © 1989, 1990 PAUL SIMON (BMI).
All Rights Reserved.*

The Boy In The Bubble
Words by Paul Simon
Music by Paul Simon and Forere Motloheloa

It was a slow day and the sun was beating
On the soldiers by the side of the road.
There was a bright light, a shattering of
    shop windows,
The bomb in the baby carriage was wired
    to the radio.
These are the days of miracle and wonder.
This is the long distance call.
The way the camera follows us in slo-mo,
The way we look to us all,
The way we look to a distant constellation
That's dying in a corner of the sky.
These are the days of miracle and wonder
And don't cry, baby, don't cry, don't cry.

It was a dry wind and it swept across
    the desert
And curled into the circle of birth.
And the dead sand was falling on
    the children,
The mothers and the fathers and the
    automatic earth.
These are the days of miracle and wonder.
This is the long distance call.
The way the camera follows us in slo-mo,
The way we look to us all,
The way we look to a distant constellation
That's dying in a corner of the sky.
These are the days of miracle and wonder
And don't cry, baby, don't cry, don't cry.

It's a turnaround jumpshot, it's everybody
    jump-start,
It's every generation throws a hero up
    the pop charts.
Medicine is magical and magical is art.
There go the boy in the bubble
And the baby with the baboon heart.
These are days of lasers in the jungle,
Lasers in the jungle somewhere.
Staccato signals of constant information,

A loose affiliation of millionaires and
    billionaires and baby:
These are the days of miracles and wonder.
This is the long distance call.
The way the camera follows us in slo-mo,
The way we look to us all, oh yeah.
The way we look to a distant constellation
That's dying in a corner of the sky.
These are the days of miracles and wonder
And don't cry, baby, don't cry, don't cry,
    don't cry.

*Copyright © 1986 PAUL SIMON (BMI).
All Rights Reserved.*

She Moves On
Paul Simon

Ooh, ooh.
I feel good,
It's a fine day,
The way the sun hits off the runway.
A cloud shifts,
The plane lifts, She moves on.
But feel the bite
Whenever you believe that
You'll be lost and love will find you,
When the road bends,
And the song ends,
She moves on.

I know the reason
I feel so blessed,
My heart still splashes
Inside my chest, but she,
She is like a top,
She cannot stop, she moves on.
A sympathetic stranger
Lights a candle in the middle of the night,
Her voice cracks,
She jumps back,
But she moves on.
She says, "Ooh, my storybook lover,
You have underestimated my power,
As you shortly will discover."
Then I fall to my knees,
Shake a rattle at the skies,
And I'm afraid that I'll be taken,
Abandoned, forsaken in her cold coffee
    eyes.

She can't sleep now,
The moon is red,
She fights a fever,
She burns in bed,
She needs to talk so,
We take a walk

Down in the maroon light.
She says, "Maybe these emotions are
As near to love as love will ever be."
So I agree.
Then the moon breaks,
She takes the corner, that's all she takes
She moves on.
She says, "Ooh, my story-book lover,
You have underestimated my power,
As you shortly will discover."
Then I fall to my knees,
I grow weak, I go slack,
As if she'd captured the breath of my
Voice in a bottle
And I can't catch it back.
But I feel good,
It's a fine day,
The way the sun hits off the runway.
A cloud shifts,
The plane lifts, She moves on.
Dit-di-li-dle la,
Dit-di-li-dle la, ooh.
Ooh.

*Copyright © 1989, 1990 PAUL SIMON (BMI).
All Rights Reserved.*

Kodachrome®
Paul Simon

When I think back
On all the crap I learned in high school,
It's a wonder
I can think at all.
And though my lack of education
Hasn't hurt me none,
I can read the writing on the wall.

Kodachrome,
They give us those nice bright colors,
They give us the greens of summers,
Makes you think all the world's
A sunny day.
Oh yeah, I got a Nikon camera,
I love to take a photograph,
So Momma, don't take my Kodachrome
    away

If you took all the girls I knew
When I was single
And brought them all together
For one night,
I know they'd never match
My sweet imagination,
Everything looks worse
In black and white

TONY CEDRAS: *KEYS/ACCORDION*

DOM CHACAL: *PERCUSSION*

CYRO BAPTISTA: *PERCUSSION*

CHRIS BOTTI: *TRUMPET*

Momma don't take my Kodachrome away.
Momma don't take my Kodachrome away.

Born at the Right Time
Paul Simon

Down among the reeds and rushes a baby
    boy was found,
His eyes as clear as centuries,
His silky hair was brown.
Never been lonely,
Never been lied to,
Never had to scuffle in fear,
Nothing denied to.
Born at the instant,
The church bells chime,
And the whole world whispering,
Born at the right time.
Me and my buddies are traveling people,
We like to go down to restaurant row.
Spend those Euro-dollars all the way from
    Washington to Tokyo.

Well, I see them in the airport lounge
Upon their mother's breast,
They follow me with open eyes,
Their uninvited guest.
Never been lonely,
Never been lied to,
Never had to scuffle in fear,
Nothing denied to.
Born at the instant,
The church bells chime,
And the whole world whispering,
Born at the right time.
Ooh, ooh, ooh, ooh, ooh.
Too many people on the bus from
    the airport,
Too many holes in the crust of the earth.
The planet groans
Every time it registers another birth.

But down among the reeds and rushes a
    baby girl was found,
Her eyes as clear as centuries,
Her silky hair was brown.
Never been lonely,
Never been lied to,
Never had to scuffle in fear,
Nothing denied to.
Born at the instant,
The church bells chime,
And the whole world whispering,

Born at the right time.
Ooh, ooh, ooh, ooh, ooh.

Train in the Distance
Paul Simon

She was beautiful as Southern skies
The night he met her.
She was married to someone.
He was doggedly determined that he would
    get her.
He was old, he was young.
From time to time he'd tip his heart,
But each time she withdrew.
Everybody loves the sound of a train in the
    distance.
Everybody thinks it's true.

Well, eventually the boy and the girl get
    married.
Sure enough they have a son.
And though they both were occupied
With the child she carried,
Disagreements had begun.
And in a while they just fell apart.
It wasn't hard to do.
Ev'rybody loves the sound of a train in the
    distance.
Ev'rybody thinks it's true.
Two disappointed believers,
Two people playing the game.
Negotiations and love songs
Are often mistaken for one and the same.

Now the man and the woman
Remain in contact,
Let us say it's for the child,
With disagreements about the meaning
Of a marriage contract,
Conversations hard and wild.
But from time to time he makes her laugh,
She cooks a meal or two.
Ev'rybody loves the sound of a train in the
    distance.
Ev'rybody thinks it's true.
Ev'rybody loves the sound of a train in the
    distance.
Ev'rybody thinks it's true.
What is the point of this story?
What information pertains?
The thought that life could be better
Is woven indelibly
Into our hearts

And our brains.
(Like a train in the distance.)

Me and Julio Down By The Schoolyard
Paul Simon

The mama pajama rolled out of bed
And she ran to the police station,
When the papa found out, he began to
    shout,
And he started the investigation.
It's against the law, it was against the law,
What the momma saw, it was against the
    law.

The mama looked down and spit on the
    ground
Ev'ry time my name gets mentioned,
The papa said, "Oy, if I get that boy
I'm gonna stick him in the house of
    detention."
Well, I'm on my way,
I don't know where I'm going,
I'm on my way,
I'm taking my time but I don't know where.
Goodbye Rosie, the Queen of Corona,
See you, me and Julio down by the
    schoolyard.
See you, me and Julio down by the
    schoolyard.

In a couple of days they come and take me
    away
But the press let the story leak,
And when the radical priest come to get me
    released,
We's all on the cover of Newsweek.
Well, I'm on my way,
I don't know where I'm going,
I'm on my way,
I'm taking my time but I don't know where.
Goodbye Rosie, the Queen of Corona,
See you, me and Julio down by the
    schoolyard.
See you, me and Julio down by the
    schoolyard.
See you, me and Julio down by the
    schoolyard.

I Know What I Know
Words by Paul Simon
Music by Paul Simon and
    General M.D. Shirinda

She looked me over and I guess she thought I
    was all right,
All right in a sort of a limited way for an off night.
She said, "Don't I know you from the
    cinematographer's party?"
I said, "Who am I to blow against the wind?"
I know what I know.
I'll sing what I said.
We come and we go.
It's a thing that I keep in the back of my head.
I know what I know
I'll sing what I said.
We come and we go.
It's a thing that I keep in the back of my head.

She said, "There's something about you that
    really reminds me of money."
She was the kind of girl who could say things
    that weren't that funny.
I said, "What does that mean, I really remind you
    of money?"
She said, "Who am I to blow against the wind?"
I know what I know.
I'll sing what I said.
We come and we go.
It's a thing that I keep in the back of my head.
I know what I know
I'll sing what I said.
We come and we go.
That's a thing that I keep in the back of my head.

She moved so easily, all I could think of was
    sunlight.
I said, "Aren't you the woman who was recently
    given a Fulbright?"
She said, "Don't I know you from the
    cinematographer's party?"
I said, "Who am I to blow against the wind?"
I know what I know.
I'll sing what I said.
We come and we go.
It's a thing that I keep in the back of my head.
I know what I know
I'll sing what I said.
We come and we go.
It's a thing that I keep in the back of my head.
I know what I know.
I know what I know.
I know what I know.

STEVE GADD: *DRUMS*

SIDINHO MOREIRA: *PERCUSSION*

VINCENT NGUINI: *GUITAR*

RAY PHIRI: *GUITAR*

The Cool, Cool River
Paul Simon

Moves like a fist through traffic,
Anger and no one can heal it,
Shoves a little bump into the momentum,
It's just a little lump,
But you feel it in the...
In the creases and the shadows,
With a rattling deep emotion.
The cool, cool river
Sweeps the wild, white ocean.
Yes Boss. The government handshake.
Yes Boss. The crusher of language.
Yes Boss. Mister Stillwater,
The face at the edge of the banquet.
The cool, the cool river.
The cool, the cool river.

I believe in the future
I may live in my car.
My radio tuned to
The voice of a star.
Song dogs barking at the break of dawn,
Lightning pushes the edges of
      a thunderstorm,
And these old hopes and fears
Still at my side.
Anger and no one can heal it,
Slides through the metal detector,
Lives like a mole in a motel,
A slide in a slide projector.
The cool, cool river
Sweeps the wild, white ocean.
The rage, the rage of love turns inward
To prayers of devotion,
These prayers are
The constant road across the wilderness.
And these prayers are,
These prayers are the memory of God,
The memory of God.

I believe in the future
We shall suffer no more.
Maybe not in my lifetime,
But in yours I feel sure.
Song dogs barking at the break of dawn,
Lightning pushes the edges of
      a thunderstorm,
And these streets,
Quiet as a sleeping army,
Send their battered dreams to heaven,
      to heaven
For the mother's restless son
Who is a witness to,

Who is a warrior
Who denies his urge to break and run,
Who says: "Hard times? I'm used to them.
The speeding planet burns, I'm used to that.
My life's so common, it disappears.
And sometimes even music
Cannot substitute for tears."

Bridge Over Troubled Water
Paul Simon

When you're weary,
Feeling small,
When tears are in your eyes,
I will dry them all.
I'm on your side.
When times get rough
And friends just can't be found,
Like a bridge over troubled water
I will lay me down.

When you're down and out,
When you're on the street,
When evening falls so hard
I will comfort you.
I'll take your part.
When darkness comes
And pain is all around,
Like a bridge over troubled water
I will lay me down.
Like a bridge over troubled water
I will lay me down.

Sail on silvergirl,
Sail on by.
Your time has come to shine.
All your dreams are on their way.
See how they shine.
If you need a friend
I'm sailing right behind.
Like a bridge over troubled water
I will ease your mind.
Like a bridge over troubled water
I will ease your mind.

Proof
Paul Simon

Soon our fortunes will be made, my darling,
And we will leave this loathsome little town.
Silver bells jingling from your black lizard
      boots, my baby,
Silver foil to trim your wedding gown.
It's true the tools of love wear down,
Time passes, a mind wanders,
It seems mindless, but it does.
Sometimes I see your face
As if through reading glasses,
And your smile seems softer than it was.

Proof.
Some people gonna call you up,
Tell you something that you already know.
Proof.
Sane people go crazy on you,
Say, "No man, that was not
The deal we made.
I got to go, I got to go."
Faith.
Faith is an island in the setting sun,
But proof, yes,
Proof is the bottom line for everyone.

My face, my race
Don't matter anymore.
My sex, my cheques
Accepted at the door.
Half moon hiding in the clouds, my darling,
And the sky is flecked with signs of hope.
Raise your weary wings against the rain,
      my baby,
Wash your tangled curls with gambler's
      soap.

Proof.
Some people gonna call you up,
Tell you something that you already know.
Proof.
Sane people go crazy on you,
Say, "No man, that was not
The deal we made.
I got to go, I got to go."
Faith.
Faith is an island in the setting sun,.
But proof, yes,
Proof is the bottom line for everyone.

The Coast
Words by Paul Simon
Music by Paul Simon and Vincent Nguini

A family of musicians took shelter for the
      night
In the little harbor church of St. Cecilia.
Two guitars, bata, bass drum and
      tambourine,
Rose of Jericho and Bougainvillea.
This is a lonely life.
Sorrows everywhere you turn.
And that's worth something when you think
      about it,
That's worth some money.
That's worth something when you think
      about it,
That's worth some money.

A trip to the market, a trip into the pearl gray
Morning sunlight that settles over
      Washington.
A trip to the market, a trip around the world
Where the evening meal is negotiable,
If there is one.
This is a lonely-lone, lonely life.
Sorrows everywhere you turn.
And that's worth something when you think
      about it,
That's worth some money.
That's worth something when you think
      about it,
That's worth some money.

To prove that I love you because I believe in
      you,
Summer skies, stars are falling all along the
      injured coast.
And if I have money, if I have children,
Summer skies, stars are falling all along the
      injured coast.
Oo-wah, oo-wah, Doo-wop a doo-wah,
Summer skies, stars are falling all along the
      injured coast.
Oo-wah, oo-wah, Doo-wop a doo-wah,
Summer skies, and the stars are falling all
      along the injured coast.

We are standing in the sunlight,
The early morning sunlight,
In the harbor church of Saint Cecilia,
To praise a soul's returning to the earth,
To the Rose of Jericho and
      the Bougainvillea.
This is the only life.

JOHN SELOLWANE: *GUITAR*

RICHARD TEE: *KEYBOARDS*

BARNEY RACHABANE:
SAXOPHONE AND PENNYWHISTLE

ARMAND SABAL-LECCO: *BASS*

And that's worth something when you think
about it,
That's worth some money.
That's worth something when you think
about it,
That's worth some money.

To prove that I love you because I believe in
you,
Summer skies, stars are falling all along the
injured coast.
And if I have money, if I have children,
Summer skies, stars are falling all along the
injured coast.
If I have weaknesses, don't let them blind
me now.
Summer skies, stars are falling all along the
injured coast.
Oo-wah, oo-wah, Doo-wop a doo-wah,
Summer skies, stars are falling.
Leaving the shadow of the valley behind me
now all along the injured coast.
Oo-wah, oo-wah, Doo-wop a doo-wah,
Summer skies and stars are falling all along
the injured coast.

Graceland
Paul Simon

The Mississippi Delta was shining like a
National guitar.
I am following the river down the highway
through the cradle of the Civil War.
I'm going to Graceland,
Graceland in Memphis, Tennessee.
I'm going to Graceland.
Poor boys and pilgrims with families
And we are going to Graceland.
My trav'ling companion is nine years old.
He is the child of my first marriage.
But I've reason to believe
We both will be received
In Graceland.

She comes back to tell me she's gone.
As if I didn't know that,
As if I didn't know my own bed,
As if I'd never noticed the way she brushed
her hair from her forehead.
And she said losing love is like a window in
your heart.
Ev'rybody sees you're blown apart,
Ev'rybody sees the wind blow.

I'm going to Graceland,
Memphis, Tennessee.
I'm going to Graceland.
Poor boys and pilgrims with families
And we are going to Graceland.
My trav'ling companions are ghosts and
empty sockets.
I'm lookin' at ghosts and empties.
But I've reason to believe we all will be
received
In Graceland.

There is a girl in New York City
Who calls herself the human trampoline,
And sometimes when I'm falling, flying or
tumbling in turmoil
I say, oh, so this is what she means.
She means we are bouncing into Graceland.
And I see losing love is like a window in your
heart.
Ev'rybody sees you're blown apart,
Ev'rybody feels the wind blow.
I'm going to Graceland, Graceland.
I'm going to Graceland.
For reasons I cannot explain,
There's some part of me wants to see
Graceland.
And I may be obliged to defend ev'ry love,
ev'ry ending
Or maybe there's no obligations, now.
Maybe I've a reason to believe we all will be
received
In Graceland.

You Can Call Me Al
Paul Simon

A man walks down the street, he says,
"Why am I soft in the middle now?
Why am I soft in the middle,
The rest of my life is so hard.
I need a photo opportunity,
I want a shot at redemption.
Don't want to end up a cartoon in a cartoon
graveyard."
Bone digger, bone digger,
Dogs in the moonlight
Far away in my well-lit door.
Mister beer belly, beer belly,
Get these mutts away from me.
I don't find this stuff amusing anymore.

If you'll be my bodyguard
I can be your long lost pal.
I can call you Betty
And Betty, when you call me,
You can call me Al.

A man walks down the street, he says,
"Why am I short of attention? Got a
Short little span of attention
And oh, my nights are so long.
Where's my wife and family?
What if I die here?
Who'll be my role model
Now that my role model is gone, gone?
He ducked back down the alley
With some roly poly little bat-faced girl.
All along, along,
There were incidents and accidents.
There are hints and allegations.

If you'll be my bodyguard
I can be your long lost pal.
I can call you Betty
And Betty, when you call me,
You can call me Al.
Call me Al.

A man walks down the street,
It's a street in a strange world.
Maybe it's the third world,
Maybe his first time around.
Doesn't speak the language.
He holds no currency.
He is a foreign man.
He is surrounded by the sound, the sound;
Cattle in the marketplace,
There's scatterings and orphanages.
He looks around, around.
He sees angels in the architecture
Spinning in infinity.
He says amen and hallelujah.

If you'll be my bodyguard
I can be your long lost pal.
I can call you Betty
And Betty, when you call me,
You can call me Al.
Call me.
Na na na na na na na na.(etc.)
Hm, hm, hm, hm, hm
If you'll be my bodyguard
I can call you Betty.

Still Crazy After All These Years
Paul Simon

I met my old lover
On the street last night;
She seemed so glad to see me,
I just smiled.
And we talked about some old times
And we drank ourselves some beers
Still crazy after all these years
Oh, still crazy after all these years.

I'm not the kind of man
Who tends to socialize;
I seem to lean on
Old familiar ways.

And I ain't no fool for love songs
That whisper in my ears
Still crazy after all these years
Oh, still crazy after all these years.

Four in the morning,
Crapped out,
Yawning;
Longing my life away.
I'll never worry;
Why should I?
It's all gonna fade.

Now I sit by my window
And I watch the cars;
I fear I'll do some damage
One fine day.
But I would not be convicted
By a jury of my peers.
Still crazy after all these years;
Oh, still crazy, still crazy,
Still crazy after all these years.

THE WATERS
(OREN, MAXINE, JULIA): *VOCALISTS*

Loves Me Like A Rock
Paul Simon

When I was a little boy,
   (When I was just a boy.)
And the devil would call my name,
   (When I was just a boy.)
I'd say, "Now who do,
Who do you think you're fooling?"
   (When I was just a boy.)

I'm a consecrated boy.
   (When I was just a boy.)
I'm a singer in the Sunday choir,
Oh, my mamma loves me,
She loves me.
She get down on her knees
And hug me like she
Loves me like a rock.

She rocks me like the rock of ages
   and loves me.
She love me, love me, love me, love me.

When I was grown to be a man,
   (Grown to be a man.)
And the devil would call my name.
   (Grown to be a man.)
I'd say, "Now who do,
Who do you think you're fooling?"
   (Grown to be a man.)

I'm a consummated man,
   (Grown to be a man.)
I can snatch a little purity,
My mamma loves me,
She loves me,
She gets down on her knees
And hug me like she
Loves me like a rock.

She rocks me like the rock of ages
   and loves me.
She love me, love me, love me, love me.

And if I was the President,
   (Was the President.)
The minute the Congress call my name.
   (Was the President.)
I say, "Now who do,
Who do you think you're fooling?"
   (Who do you think you're fooling?)

I've got the Presidential Seal,
   (Was the President.)
I'm up on the Presidential Podium.
My mama loves me,
She loves me.
She get down on her knees
And hug me like she
Loves me like a rock.

She rocks me like the rock of ages
   and loves me.
She love me, love me, love me, love me.
   (Love me like a rock.)
She love me, love me, love me, love me.
   (Love me like a rock.)
She love me, love me, love me, love me.

Diamonds On The Soles
Of Her Shoes
Words and Music by Paul Simon
Beginning by Paul Simon
   and Joseph Shabalala

(Awa awa) Odez enzuene zanam chinge.
(Awa awa) Si bona nenze ge gyja.
(Awa awa) Amantu mezane, aya.
She's a rich girl, she don't try to hide it;
Diamonds on the soles of her shoes.
He's a poor boy, empty as a pocket,
Empty as a pocket with nothing to lose.
Sing ta na na, ta na na na.
She got diamonds on the soles of her shoes.
Ta na na, ta na na na.
She got diamonds on the soles of her shoes,
Diamonds on the soles of her shoes,
Diamonds on the soles of her shoes,
Diamonds on the soles of her shoes.

People say she's crazy, she got diamonds on
  the soles of her shoes.
Well, that's one way to lose these walking
  blues,
Diamonds on the soles of her shoes.
She was physic'lly forgotten,
And then she slipped into my pocket with
  my car keys.
She said, "You've taken me for granted
  because I please you,
Wearing these diamonds."
And I could say oo.
As if ev'rybody knows what I'm talking
  about.
As if ev'rybody here would know exactly
  what I was talking about.
Talkin' 'bout diamonds on the soles
  of her shoes.

She makes the sign of the teaspoon,
He makes the sign of the wave.
The poor boy changes clothes and he puts
  on after shave
To compensate for his ordinary shoes.
And she said, "Honey, take me dancing,
But they ended up by sleeping in a doorway
By the bodegas and the lights on
  upper Broadway,
Wearing diamonds on the soles
  of their shoes.
And I could say oo.
And ev'rybody knows what I'm talking
about.
I mean ev'rybody here would know exactly
what I was talking about.
Talkin' 'bout diamonds on the soles of her
shoes.

People say I'm crazy,
I got diamonds on the soles of my shoes.
Well, that's one way to lose these
  walking blues.
Diamonds on the soles of my shoes.
Ta na na na,
Ta na na na na. (etc.)

Copyright © 1986 PAUL SIMON (BMI).
All Rights Reserved.

Hearts and Bones
Paul Simon

One and one-half wandering Jews,
Free to wander wherever they choose,
Are traveling together
In the Sangre de Cristo,
The Blood of Christ Mountains
Of New Mexico,
On the last leg of a journey
They started a long time ago,

The arc of a love affair,
Rainbows in the high desert air.
Mountain passes slipping into stones,
Hearts and bones,
Hearts and bones,
Hearts and bones.

Thinking back to the season before,
Looking back through the cracks
  in the door,
Two people were married.
The act was outrageous.
The bride was contagious.
She burned like a bride.
These events may have had some effect
On the man with the girl by his side,

The arc of a love affair,
His hands rolling down her hair.
Love like lightning shaking till it moans.
Hearts and bones,
Hearts and bones,
Hearts and bones.

And whoa whoa whoa,
She said, "Why?
Why don't we drive through the night,
And we'll wake up down in Mexico?
Oh I,
I don't know nothin' about,
Nothin' about no Mexico.

Tell me why,
Why won't you love me
For who I am
Where I am?"
He said,
"'Cause that's not the way the world is,
  baby.
This is how I love you, baby.
This is how I love you, baby."

One and one-half wandering Jews
Returned to their natural coasts
To resume old acquaintances,
Step out occasionally
And speculate who had been damaged
  the most
Easy time will determine if these
  consolations
Will be their reward,

The arc of a love affair,
Waiting to be restored.
You take two bodies and you twirl them
  into one,
Their hearts and their bones,
And they won't come undone,
Hearts and bones,
Hearts and bones,
Hearts and bones,
Hearts and bones.

Copyright © 1982, 1983 PAUL SIMON (BMI).
All Rights Reserved.

Late In The Evening
Paul Simon

The first thing I remember,
I was lying in my bed.
I couldn't of been no more
Than one or two.
I remember there's a radio
Comin' from the room next door,
And my mother laughed
They way some ladies do
When it's late in the evening
And the music's seeping through.

The next thing I remember,
I am walking down the street.
I'm feeling all right.
I'm with my boys.
I'm with my troops, yeah.
Down along the avenue,
Some guys were shootin' pool,
And I heard the sound
Of a cappella groups, yeah,
Singing late in the evening,
And all the girls out on the stoops, yeah.

Then I learned to play some lead guitar.
I was underage in this funky bar.
And I stepped outside to smoke myself a "J."
And when I came back to the room,
Everybody just seemed to move,
And I turned my amp up loud, and I began
  to play.
And it was late in the evening,
And I blew that room away.

The first thing I remember
When you came into my life,
I said, "I'm gonna get that girl
No matter what I do."
Well, I guess I'd been in love before,
And once or twice I been on the floor,
But I never loved no one
The way that I loved you.
And it was late in the evening,
And all the music seeping through.

Copyright © 1978, 1980 PAUL SIMON (BMI).
All Rights Reserved.

America
Paul Simon

"Let us be lovers,
We'll marry our fortunes together.
I've got some real estate
Here in my bag."
So we bought a pack of cigarettes,
And Mrs. Wagner's pies,

And walked off
To look for America.
"Kathy," I said,
As we boarded a Greyhound in Pittsburgh,
"Michigan seems like a dream to me now.
It took me four days
To hitchhike from Saginaw.
I've come to look for America."

Laughing on the bus,
Playing games with the faces,
She said the man in the gabardine suit
Was a spy.
I said, "Be careful,
His bowtie is really a camera."
"Toss me a cigarette,
I think there's one in my raincoat."
"We smoked the last one
An hour ago."

So I looked at the scenery.
She read her magazine;
And the moon rose over an open field.
"Kathy, I'm lost," I said,
Though I knew she was sleeping.
"I'm empty and aching and
I don't know why."
Counting the cars
On the New Jersey Turnpike.
They've all come
To look for America,
All come to look for America.

Copyright © 1968 PAUL SIMON (BMI).
All Rights Reserved.

The Boxer
Paul Simon

I am just a poor boy.
Though my story's seldom told,
I have squandered my resistance
For a pocketful of mumbles,
Such are promises.
All lies and jest,
Still a man hears what he wants to hear,
And disregards the rest.

When I left my home
And my family,
I was no more than a boy
In the company of strangers
In the quiet of the railway station
Running scared,
Laying low,
Seeking out the poorer quarters
Where the ragged people go,
Looking for the places
Only they would know.
Lie la lie (etc.)

Asking only workman's wages
I come looking for a job,
But I get no offers,
Just a come-on from the whores on Seventh
  Avenue.
I do declare,
There were times when I was so lonesome
I took some comfort there.
Lie la lie (etc.)

Then I'm laying out my winter clothes
And wishing I was gone,
Going home
Where the New York City winters
Aren't bleeding me,
Leading me,
Going home.

In the clearing stands a boxer,
And a fighter by his trade,
And he carries the reminders
Of ev'ry glove that laid him down
Or cut him till he cried out
In his anger and his shame,
"I am leaving, I am leaving,"
But the fighter still remains.
Lie la lie (etc.)

Copyright © 1968 PAUL SIMON (BMI).
All Rights Reserved.

Cecilia
Paul Simon

Celia, you're breaking my heart,
You're shaking my confidence daily.
Oh, Cecilia, I'm down on my knees,
I'm begging you please to come home.

Making love in the afternoon with Cecilia,
Up in my bedroom,
I got up to wash my face.
When I come back to bed,
Someone's taken my place.

Celia, you're breaking my heart,
You're shaking my confidence daily.
Oh, Cecilia, I'm down on my knees.
I'm begging you please to come home.
Come on home,
Poh poh poh poh. (etc.)

Jubilation, she loves me again,
I fall on the floor and I laughing.
Jubilation, she loves me again,
I fall on the floor and I laughing.
Oh oh oh oh oh oh oh oh oh oh
Oh oh oh oh oh oh oh oh oh oh
Come on home.

Copyright © 1969 PAUL SIMON (BMI).
All Rights Reserved.

The Sound Of Silence
Paul Simon

Hello darkness, my old friend,
I've come to talk with you again,
Because a vision softly creeping,
Left its seeds while I was sleeping,
And the vision that was planted in my brain
Still remains
Within the sound of silence.

In restless dreams I walked alone,
Narrow streets of cobblestone,
'Neath the halo of a street lamp,
I turned my collar to the cold and damp
When my eyes were stabbed by the flash
  of a neon light
That split the night
And touched the sound of silence.

And in the naked light I saw
Ten thousand people, maybe more.
People talking without speaking,
People hearing without listening,
People writing songs that voices never share
And no one dare
Disturb the sound of silence.

"Fools," said I, "you do not know,
Silence like a cancer grows."
"Hear my words that I might teach you,
Take my arms that I might reach you."
But my words like silent rain-drops fell,
And echoed in the wells of silence.

And the people bowed and prayed
to the neon god they made.
And the sign flashed its warning
In the words that it was forming.
And the signs said "The words of the
prophets are written
on the subway walls
And tenement halls,"
And whispered in the sounds of silence.

Copyright © 1964 PAUL SIMON (BMI).
All Rights Reserved.

Front cover photograph by Kevin Coughlin
Back cover photograph by Nick Elgar
Interior photographs by Yann Gamblin and Eighty/Twenty Inc.

Order No. PS 11261
US International Standard Book Number: 0.8256.1337.X
UK International Standard Book Number: 0.7119.2932.7

Exclusive Distributors:
Music Sales Corporation
257 Park Avenue South, New York, NY 10010 USA
Music Sales Limited
8/9 Frith Street, London W1V 5TZ England
Music Sales Pty. Limited
120 Rothschild Street, Rosebery, Sydney, NSW 2018, Australia

Printed in the United States of America by
Vicks Lithograph and Printing Corporation

Contents

The Obvious Child

Words and Music by PAUL SIMON

14

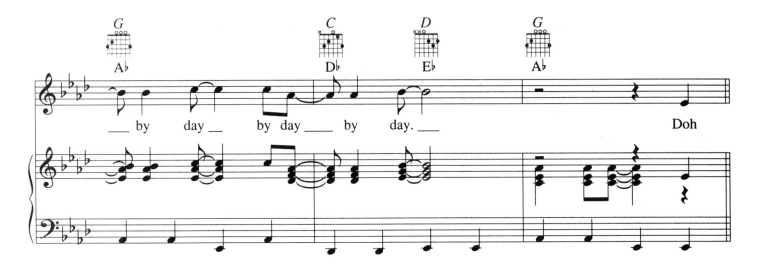

by day __ by day ___ by day. ___ Doh

doh, _____ Doh doh. _____ Doh

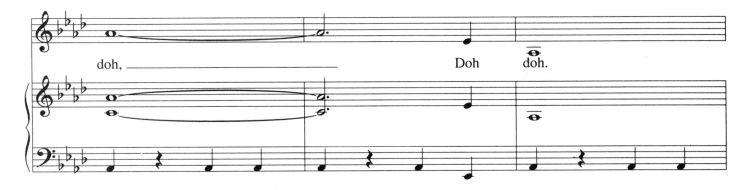

doh, _____ Doh doh.

2. Well, I've been wak- ing up at sun - rise, I've been fol- low- ing the

16

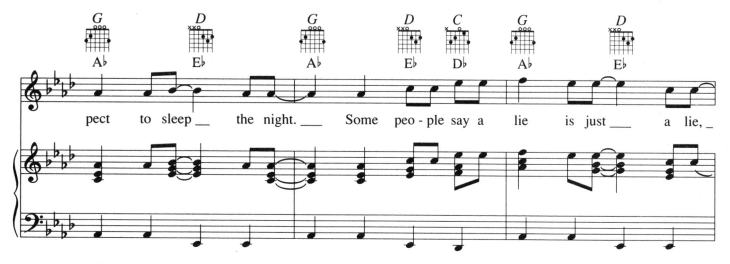

The Boy In The Bubble

Words by PAUL SIMON
Music by PAUL SIMON and FORERE MOTLOHELOA

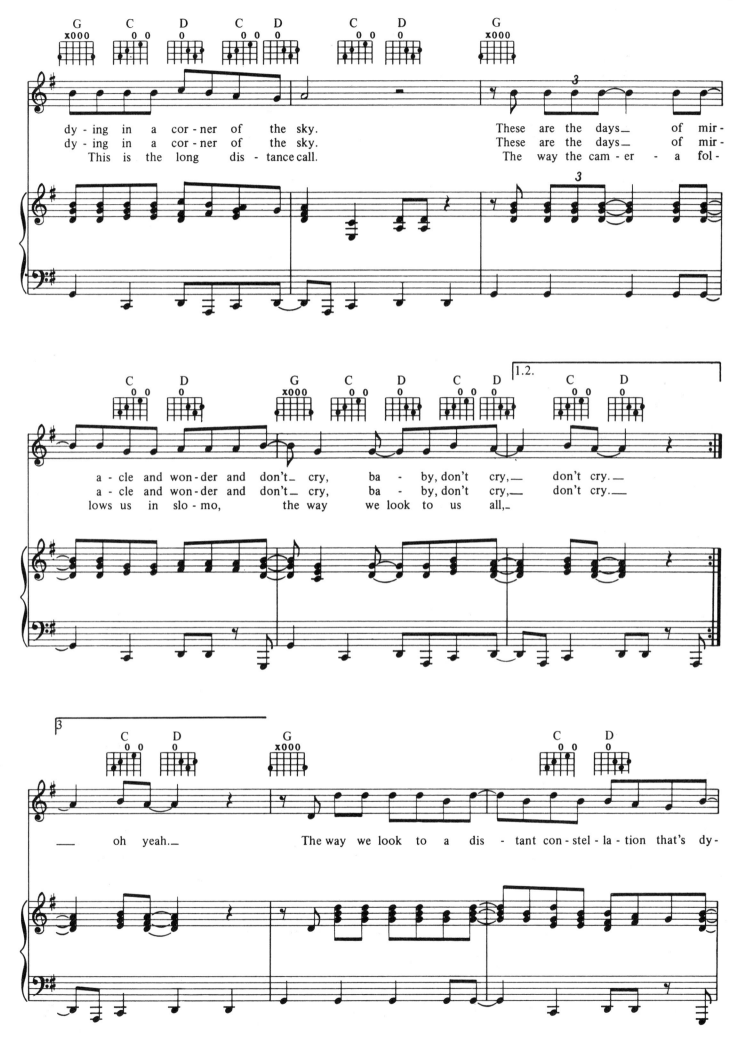

She Moves On

Words and Music by PAUL SIMON

Moderately bright

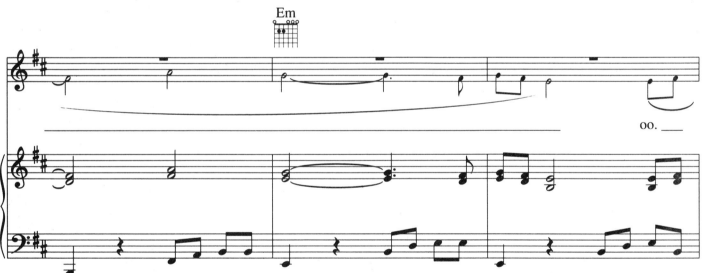

1. I feel good, ___ It's a fine day, ___ The way the sun hits off the run - way. _____ A cloud __ shifts, The plane __

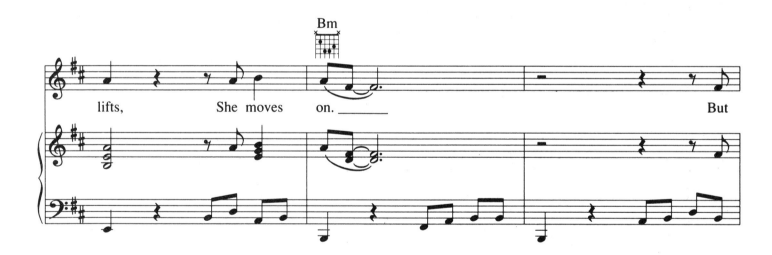

lifts, She moves on. _____ But

feel the bite _ When- ev - er you be- lieve ____ that You'll be lost and love will

find you,   When the road ___ bends,   And the song __

ends, ___   She moves _____ on. _____

Instrumental

28

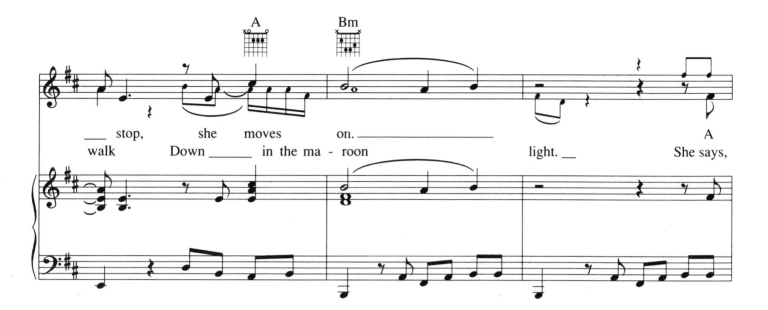

___ stop, she moves on. _____ A
walk Down _____ in the ma - roon light. __ She says,

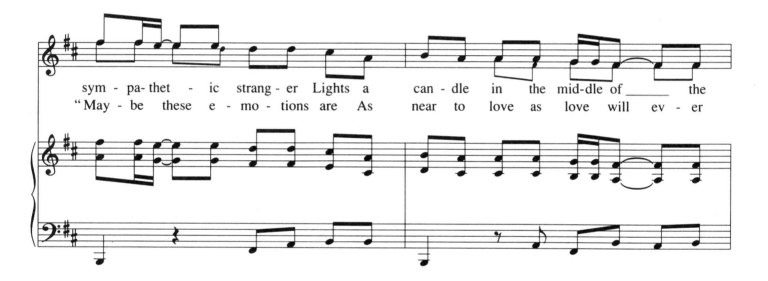

sym - pa-thet - ic strang - er Lights a can - dle in the mid-dle of _____ the
"May - be these e - mo - tions are As near to love as love will ev - er

night, _____ Her voice __ cracks, She jumps
be." _____ So I a - gree. Then the moon _ breaks, She takes the

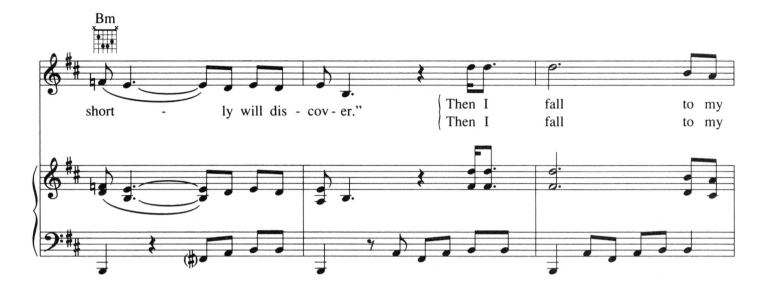

short - ly will dis - cov - er." | Then I fall to my
| Then I fall to my

knees, Shake a rat - tle at the skies, And I'm a-
knees, I grow weak, _____ I go slack, ____ As if she'd

fraid that I'll _ be tak - en, a - ban - doned, _ for - sak - en in her
cap - tured the breath of my Voice in a bot - tle And I

cold   cof - fee   eyes. _____
can't   catch it

3. She can't

back.   But I   feel   good,   It's a fine

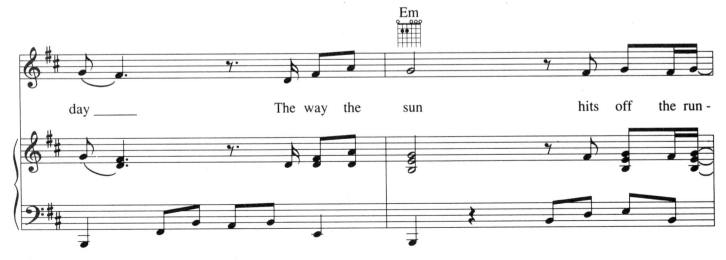

day _____   The way the   sun   hits off   the run -

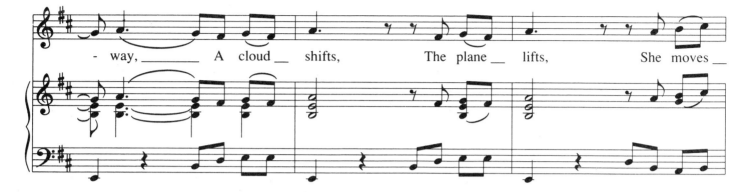

- way, _____ A cloud __ shifts, The plane __ lifts, She moves __

on. _____ Dit - di - li - dle la,

Dit - di - li - dle la, ooh. _____ Ooh. __

repeat and fade

Kodachrome®

Words and Music by PAUL SIMON

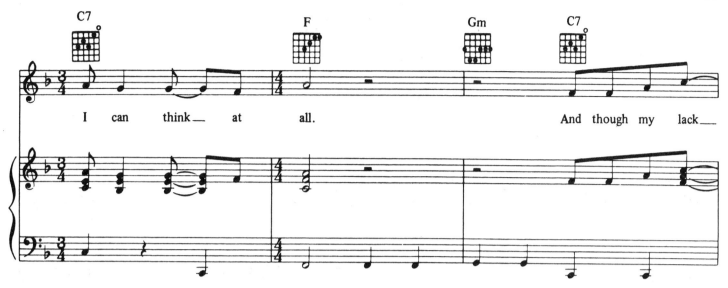

I can think_ at all.   And though my lack_

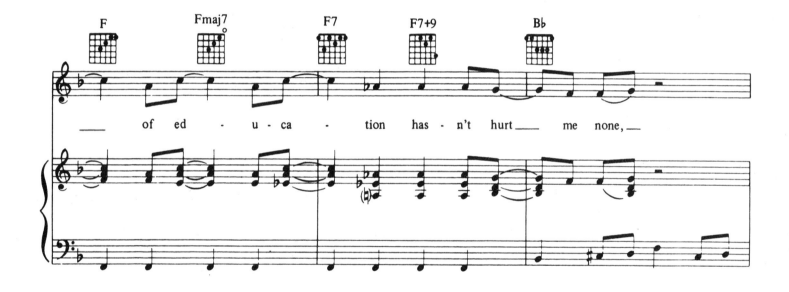

_ of ed - u - ca - tion has - n't hurt_ me none,

I can read the writ - ing on the wall._

36

And brought them all to-geth - er for ___ one

night,

I know they'd nev - er match ___ my

sweet im - ag - i - na - tion, ___

And ev - 'ry - thing looks worse in black and white. Ko - da -

D.S. al Fine

Proof

Words and Music by PAUL SIMON

Soon _____ our for- tunes _____ will be made, _____ my dar-
It's true the tools of love __ wear down,

ling, And we will leave this loath- some _____ lit- tle town. _
Time pass- es, A mind wan- ders, It seems mind- less, but it does. __

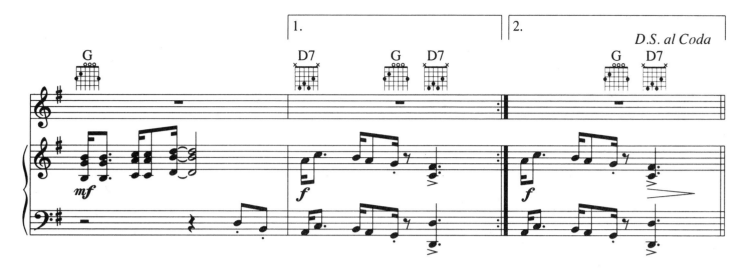

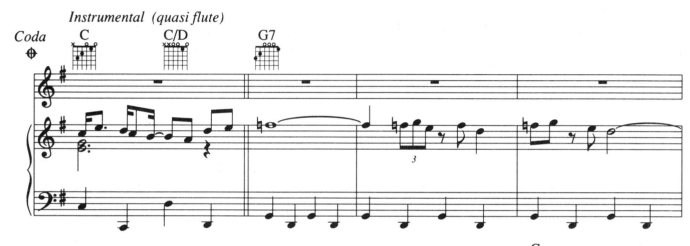

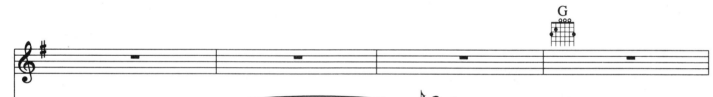

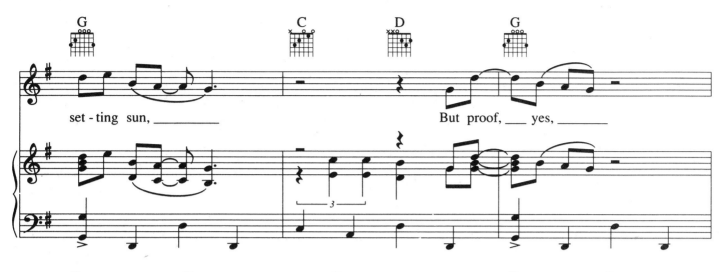

set - ting sun, _____ But proof, ___ yes, _____

Proof __ is the bot-tom line __ for ev - ery-one.

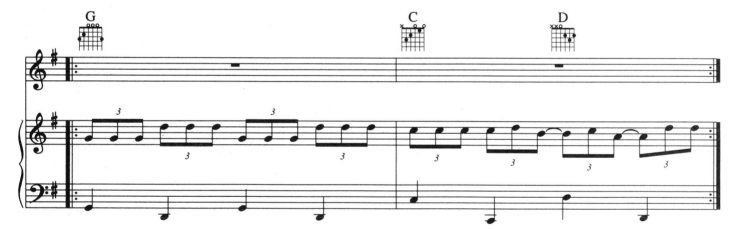

He - lah, wa - he - la a ton - ga he, he - la.

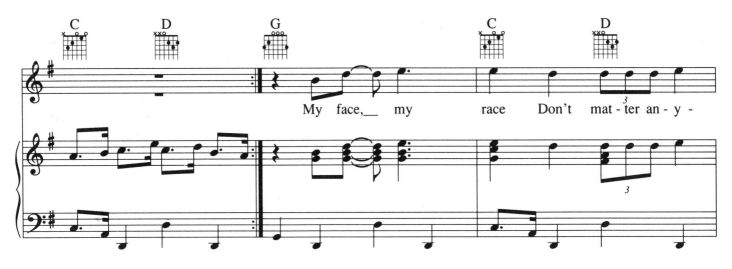

My face,__ my race Don't mat - ter an - y -

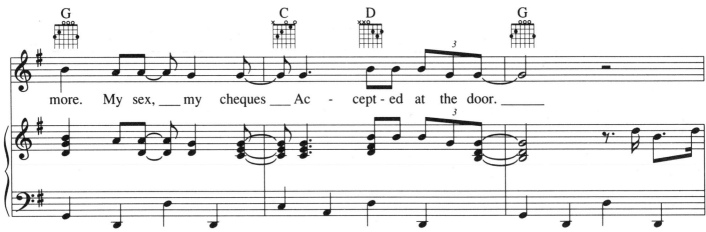

more. My sex,___ my cheques ___ Ac - cept - ed at the door. _____

poco a poco cresc.

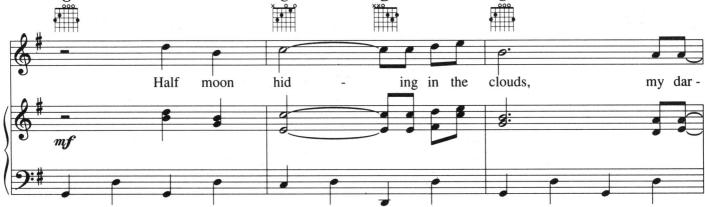

Half moon hid - ing in the clouds, my dar -

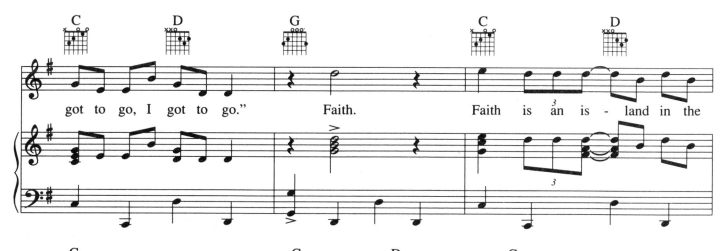

got to go, I got to go." Faith. Faith is an is - land in the

set - ting sun, _____ But proof, ___ yes, _____

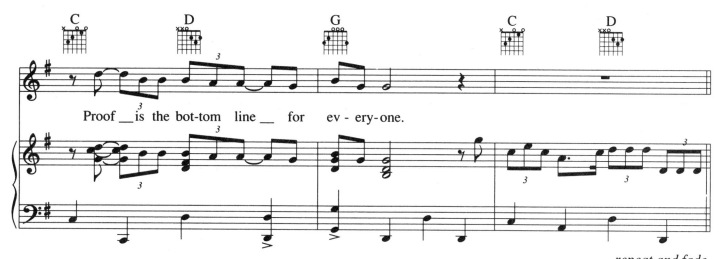

Proof __ is the bot - tom line __ for ev - ery-one.

repeat and fade

He - lah, wa - he - la a ton - ga he he - la.

Born At The Right Time

Words and Music by PAUL SIMON

Me and my bud-dies we are trav-el-ling peo-ple, We like to go down to res-tau-rant row.

Spend those Eu - ro-dol - lars

all the way from Wash-ing- ton _____ to To - ky-o. _____ 2. Well, I

Train In The Distance

Words and Music by PAUL SIMON

She was beau - ti - ful as
Well, e - ven - tu - 'lly the
Now the man ____ and the

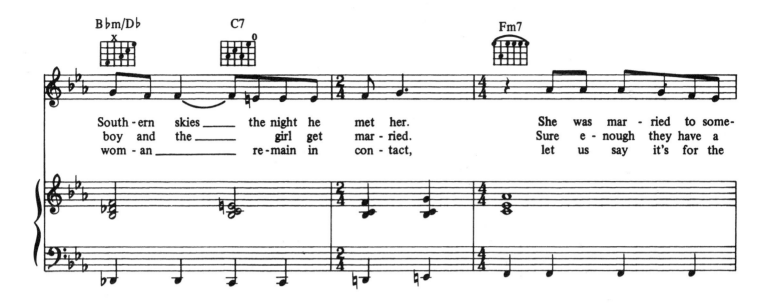

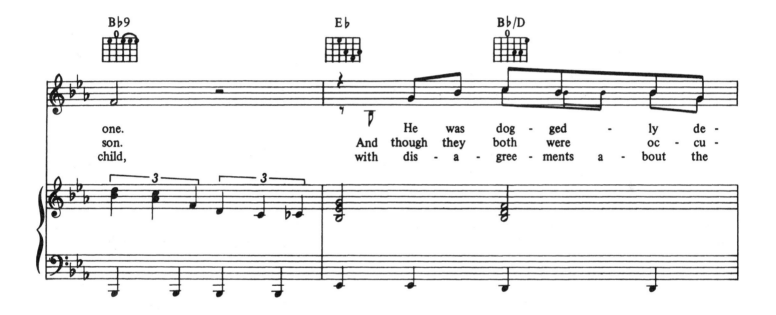

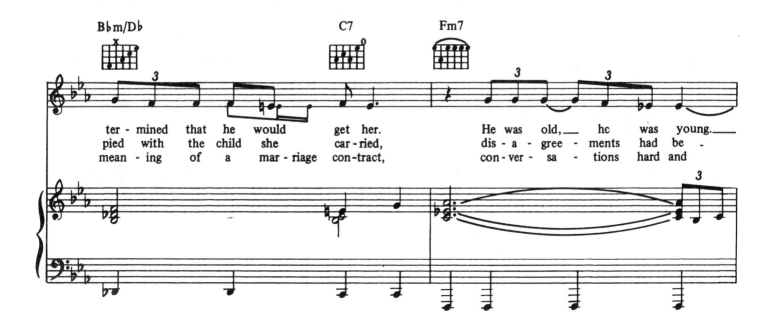

love__ songs__ are of - ten mis - tak - en_ for one and the same.__
bet - ter__ is wo - ven_ in - del - i - bly in - to our hearts__

Coda

D. S. 𝄋 *(no repeats) al Coda*

and our brains._

(Like a train_ in the dis - tance.)

Repeat and fade

Me And Julio Down By The Schoolyard

Words and Music by PAUL SIMON

men - tioned,
leak,

The pa - pa said, "Oy, if I
And when the rad - i - cal priest come to

get that boy___ I'm gon - na stick him in the house of de - ten -
get me re - leased,___ we's all on the cov - er of News -

No chord

- tion."
- week.

Well, I'm on my way,___

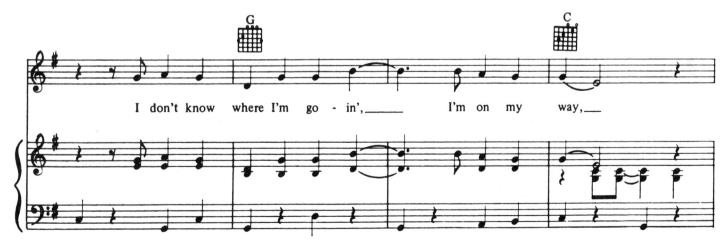

I don't know where I'm go - in',___ I'm on my way,___

I'm tak - in' my time___ but I don't know where.___ Good - bye

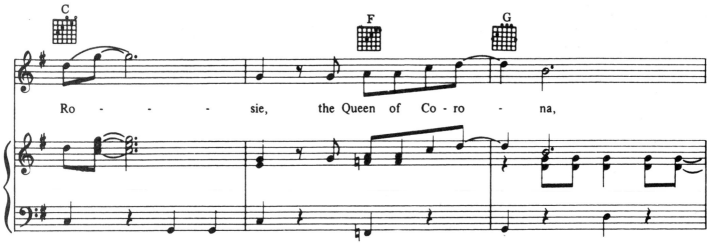

Ro - - - sie, the Queen of Co - ro - na,

See you, Me And Ju - lio Down By The School - yard.___

See you, Me And Ju - lio

63

I Know What I Know

Words by PAUL SIMON
Music by PAUL SIMON and GENERAL M.D. SHIRINDA

looked me o - ver and I guess she thought I was all right, all
some - thing a - bout you that real - ly re - minds me of mon - ey." She was the
moved so eas - i - ly, all I could think of was sun - light. I said,

G   C   F

right   in   a   sort   of   a   lim-it-ed   way__ for   an   off   night.   She said,
kind   of   a   girl   who   could   say   things   that   were-n't   that   fun-ny.   I   said,
"Are-n't   you   the   wom-an   who   was   re-cent-ly   giv-en   a   Ful-bright?"   She said,

"Don't   I   know__ you   from   the   cin-e-mat-o-graph-er's   par - ty?"   I   said,
"What   does   that__   mean,   I   real-ly   re-mind   you   of   mon - ey?"   She said,
"Don't   I   know   you   from   the   cin-e-mat-o-graph-er's   par - ty?"   I   said,

"Who   am   I   to   blow   a - gainst__ the   wind?"__ ⎫
"Who   am   I   to   blow   a - gainst__ the   wind?"__ ⎬   I   know   what   I___   know.__
"Who   am   I   to   blow   a - gainst__ the   wind?"__ ⎭

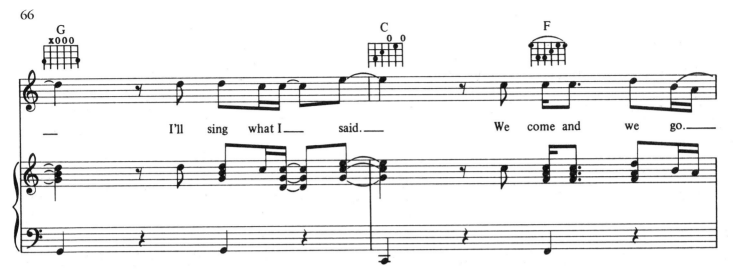

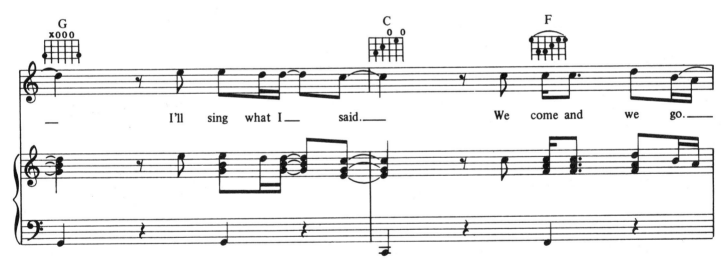

The Cool, Cool River

Words and Music by PAUL SIMON

heav - en,   to heav - en   For the moth-er's rest - less

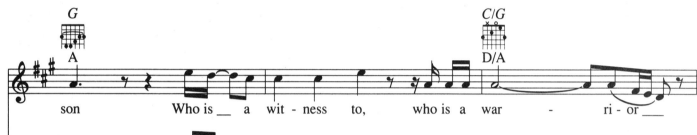

son   Who is _ a wit - ness to,   who is a war - ri - or __

Who de - nies his urge _ to   break _ and run, _ Who says: "Hard times? ____ I'm used to them.

The speed-ing plan-et burns, I'm used to that. My life's __ so com-mon, it dis-ap-

pears. And some-times _____ e-ven mu-sic _____

Can-not sub-sti-tute for ___ tears." _____

repeat and fade

Bridge Over Troubled Water

Words and Music by PAUL SIMON

The Coast

Words by PAUL SIMON
Music by PAUL SIMON and VINCENT NGUINI

fam - i - ly of mu - si - cians took shel - ter for the night __ In the
trip to the mar - ket, a trip in - to the pearl gray

lit-tle   har - bor church of Saint Ce - cil   - ia.
morn-ing   sun - light that set - tles   o - ver   Wash - ing - ton.

Two gui - tars,   ba - ta, bass drum _____ and tarm - bou - rine, __
A   trip to the   mar - ket,   a   trip a - round the world   Where the

Rose of Jer - i - cho and Bou - gain - vil - lea.
eve - ning meal is ne - go - ti - able, if there is one.

This is a

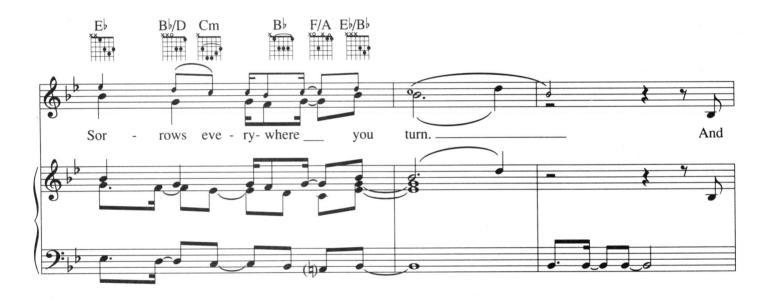

This is a lone - ly life.
lone - ly - lone, ___ lone-ly life.

Sor - rows eve - ry - where ___ you turn. _____ And

that's worth ___ some - thing when you think a - bout it, That's worth ___ some mon-ey.

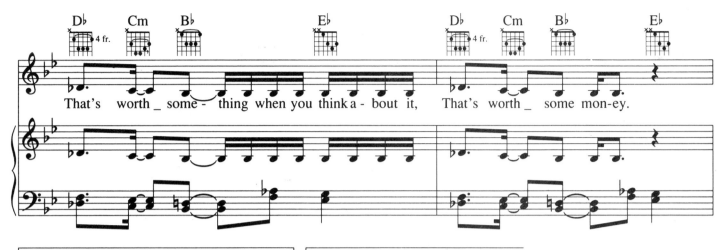

That's worth _ some - thing when you think a - bout it, That's worth _ some mon - ey.

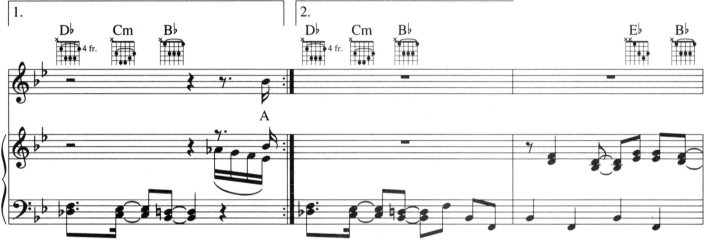

1.

2.

A

To prove _ that I love you be - cause __ I be - lieve in you,
And if __ I have mon -ey, _____ if ___ I have chil - dren,

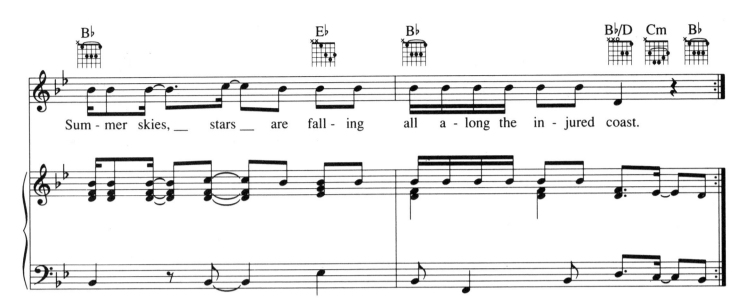

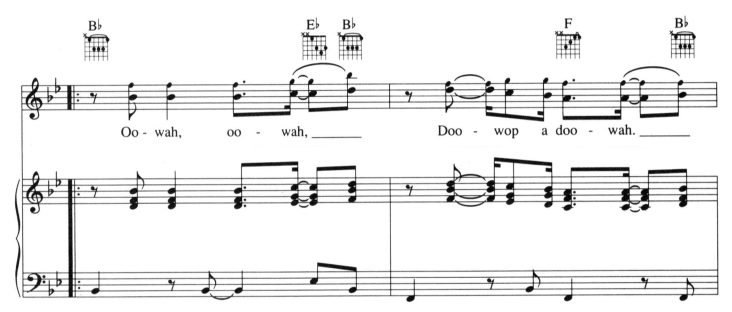

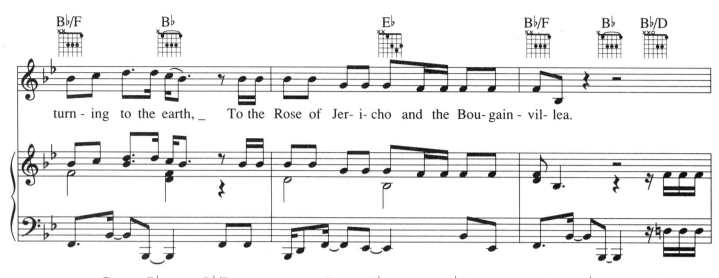

turn - ing to the earth, _ To the Rose of Jer- i- cho and the Bou- gain - vil- lea.

This is the on - ly life.

And

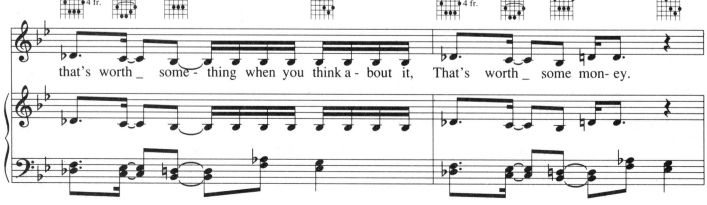

that's worth _ some - thing when you think a - bout it, That's worth _ some mon - ey.

That's worth _ some - thing when you think a - bout it, That's worth _ some mon - ey.

To prove _ that I love you   be - cause _ I be - lieve in you,
And if _ I have mon - ey, _____   if ___ I have chil - dren,

Leav - ing the shad - ow of the val - ley be - hind me now __

all a - long the in - jured coast.

Oo - wah, oo - wah, _____ Doo - wop a doo - wah. _____

repeat and fade

Sum - mer skies __ and stars __ are fall - ing all a - long the in - jured coast.

Graceland

Words and Music by PAUL SIMON

The Mis-sis-sip-pi Del-ta was shin-ing like a Na-tion-al gui-tar. I am fol-low-ing the riv-er down the high-way through the cra-dle of the Civ-il War. I'm go-ing to Grace-

land, Grace - land in Mem-phis, Ten - nes - see. I'm go - ing to Grace - land.
land, Mem-phis, Ten - nes - see. I'm go - ing to Grace - land.
land, Grace - land. I'm go - ing to Grace - land.

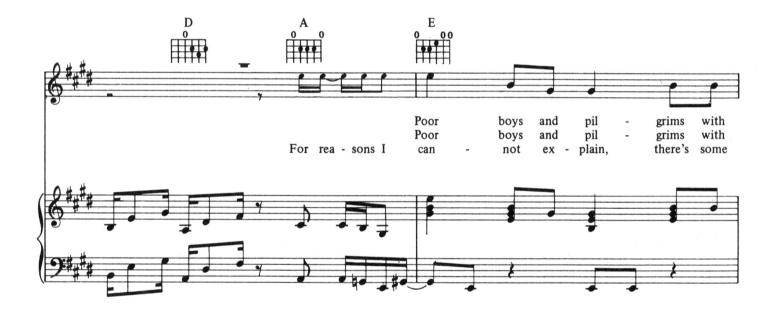

Poor boys and pil - grims with
Poor boys and pil - grims with
For rea - sons I can - not ex - plain, there's some

fam - i - lies__ and we are go - ing to Grace - land.
fam - i - lies__ and we are go - ing to Grace - land.
part of__ me wants to see Grace - land.

My trav - 'ling com - pan - ion is
My trav - 'ling com - pan - ions are
And I may be o - bliged to de - fend ev - 'ry

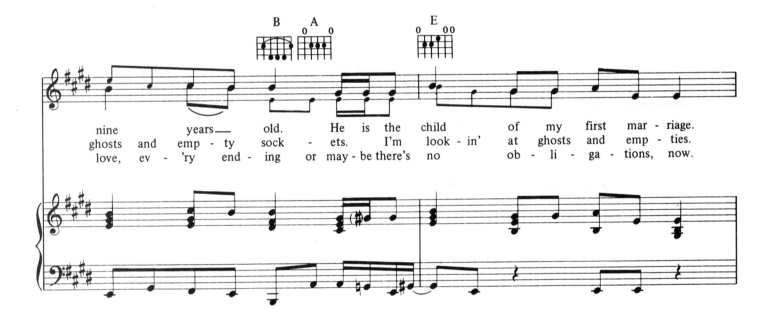

nine years___ old. He is the child of my first mar - riage.
ghosts and emp - ty sock - ets. I'm look - in' at ghosts and emp - ties.
love, ev - 'ry end - ing or may - be there's no ob - li - ga - tions, now.

But I've rea - son to be - lieve we both___
But I've rea - son to be - lieve we all___
May - be I've a rea - son to be - lieve we all___

will be re - ceived in Grace - land.
will be re - ceived in Grace - land.
will be re - ceived in Grace - land.

She comes back to tell me she's gone.
There is a girl in New York Cit - y who

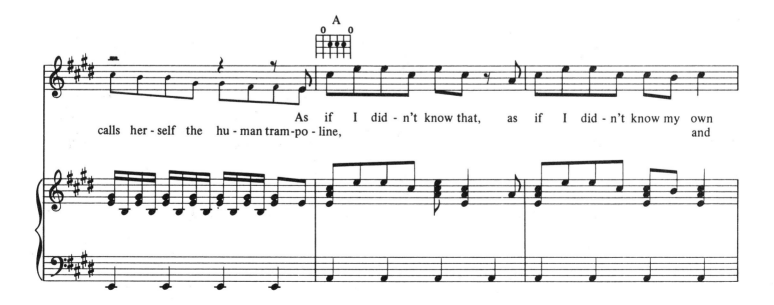

As if I did - n't know that, as if I did - n't know my own
calls her - self the hu - man tram - po - line, and

You Can Call Me Al

Words and Music by PAUL SIMON

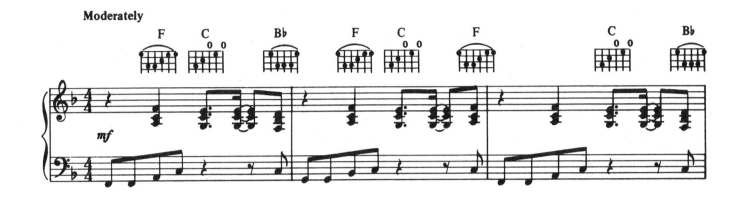

Moderately

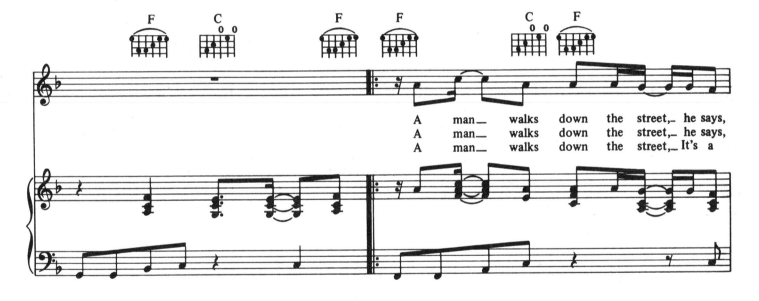

A man__ walks down the street,__ he says,
A man__ walks down the street,__ he says,
A man__ walks down the street,__ It's a

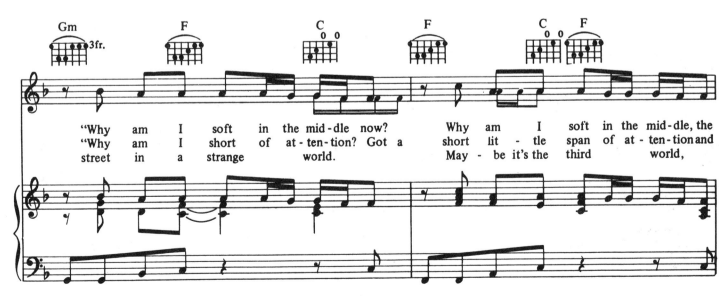

"Why am I soft in the mid-dle now? Why am I soft in the mid-dle, the
"Why am I short of at-ten-tion? Got a short lit-tle span of at-ten-tion and
street in a strange world. May-be it's the third world,

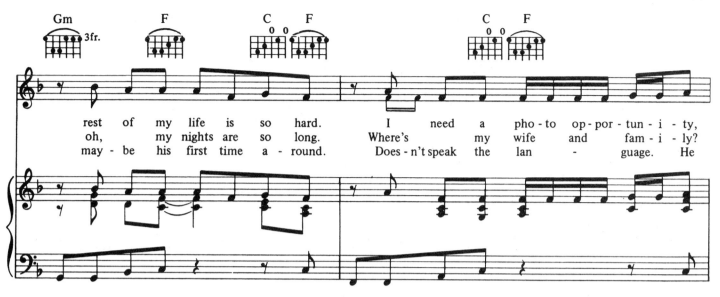

rest of my life is so hard.
oh, my nights are so long.
may - be his first time a - round.

I need a pho - to op - por - tun - i - ty,
Where's my wife and fam - i - ly?
Does - n't speak the lan - guage. He

I want a shot at re - demp - tion. Don't want to end up a car - toon in a
What if I die here? Who'll be my role mod - el
holds no cur - ren - cy. He is a for - eign man.

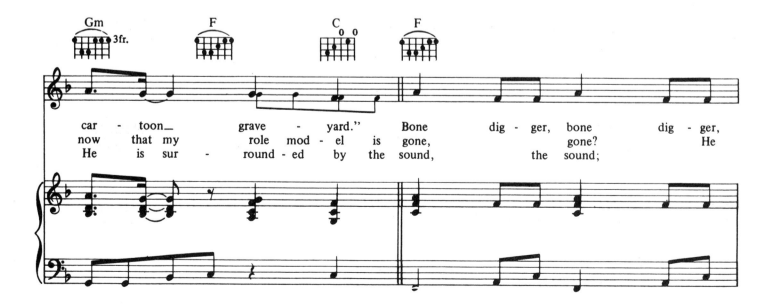

car - toon____ grave - yard." Bone dig - ger, bone dig - ger,
now that my role mod - el is gone, gone? He
He is sur - round - ed by the sound, the sound;

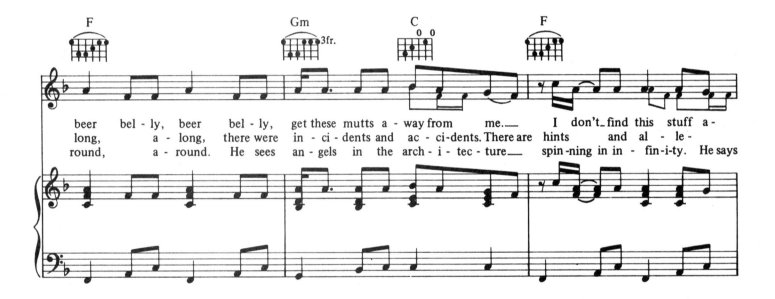

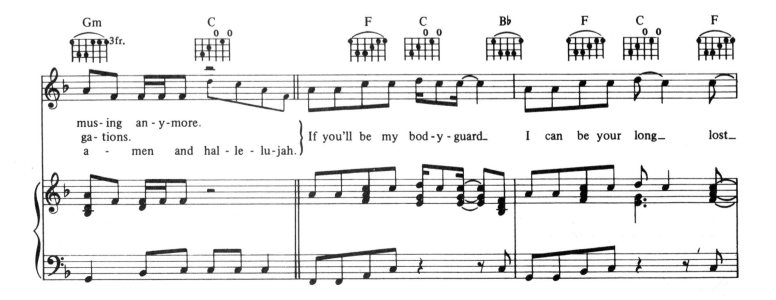

pal.

I can call you Bet - ty and

Bet - ty, when you call me, you can call me Al.

call me Al. ___ Call me Al.

To Coda ⊕

1.

2.

Tacet

D.C. al Coda ⊕

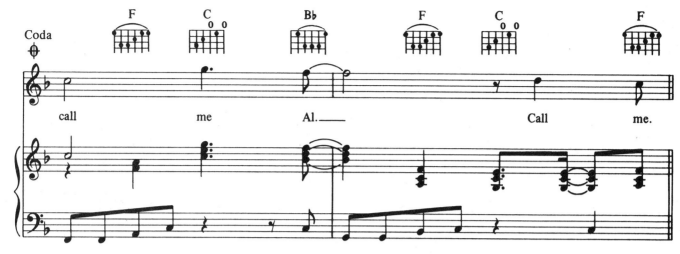

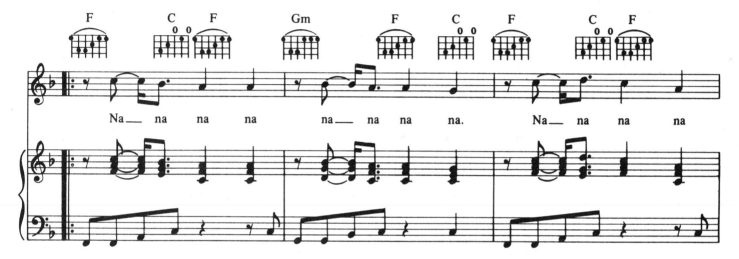

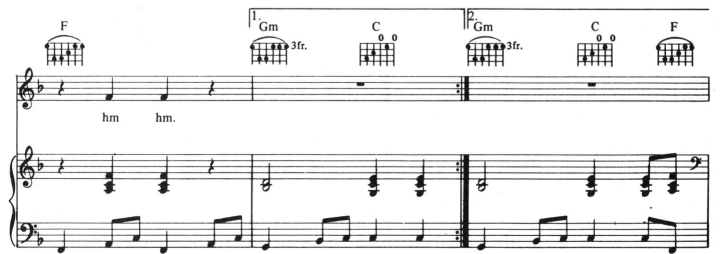

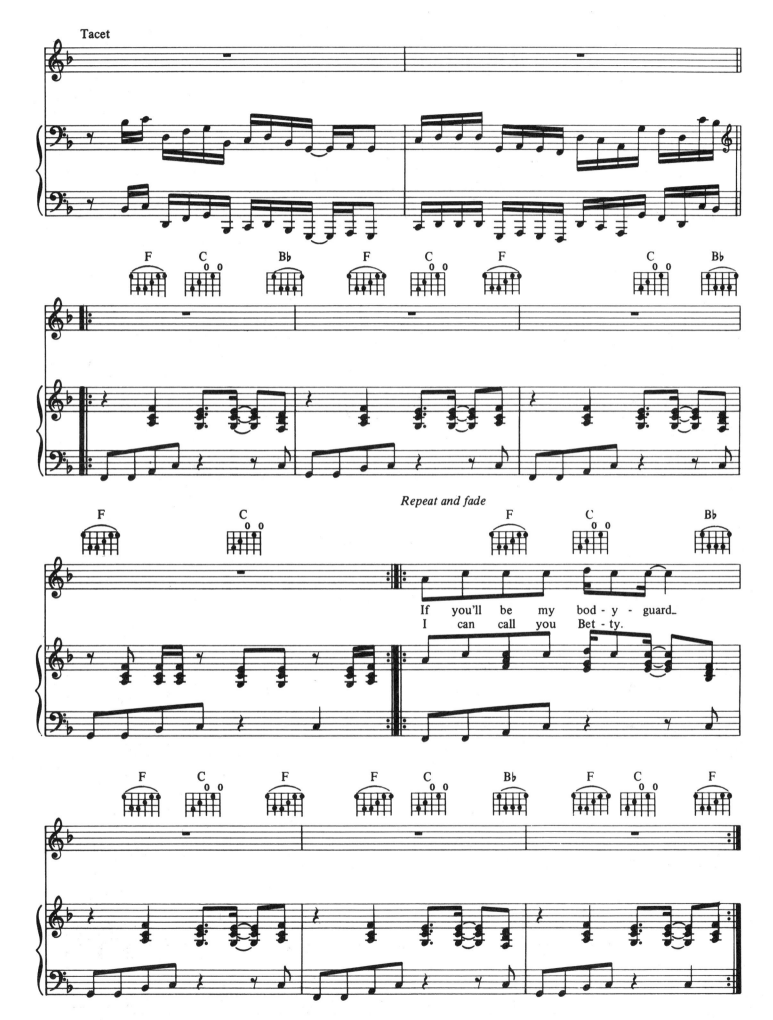

Still Crazy After All These Years

Words and Music by PAUL SIMON

108

Loves Me Like A Rock

Words and Music by PAUL SIMON

Diamonds On The Soles Of Her Shoes

Words and Music by PAUL SIMON
Beginning by PAUL SIMON and JOSEPH SHABALALA

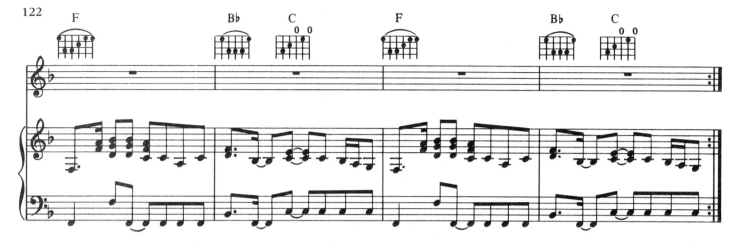

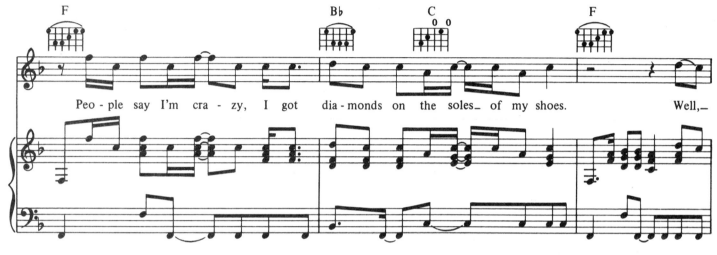

Peo - ple say I'm cra - zy, I got dia - monds on the soles_ of my shoes. Well,—

that's one way to lose these walk-ing blues. Dia-monds on the soles_ of my shoes.

Repeat and fade

Ta na na na na, ta na na na na.

The Sound Of Silence

Words and Music by PAUL SIMON

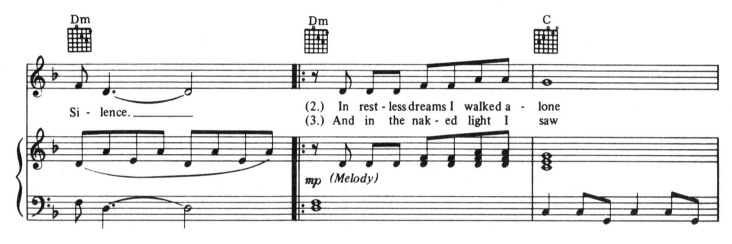

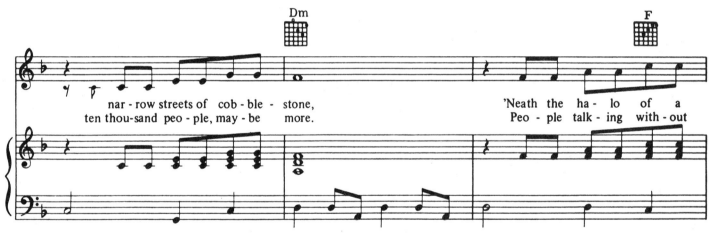

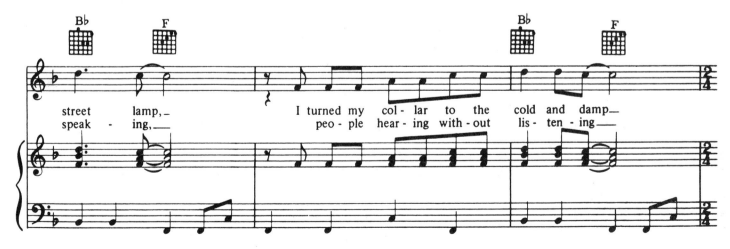

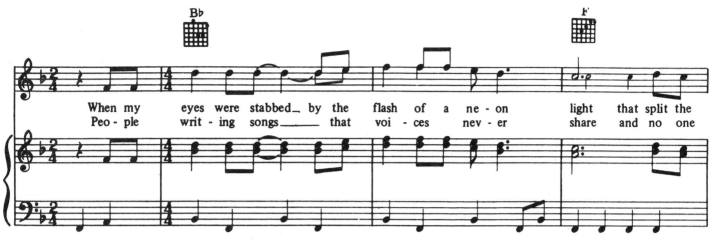

When my eyes were stabbed by the flash of a ne - on light that split the
Peo - ple writ - ing songs that voi - ces nev - er share and no one

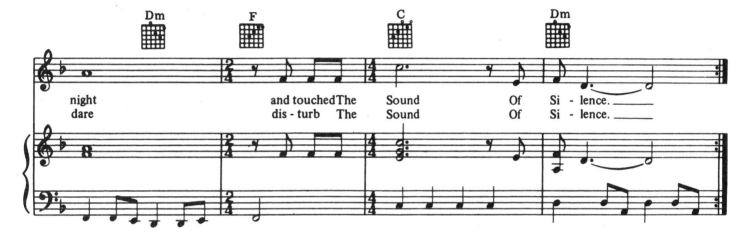

night and touched The Sound Of Si - lence.
dare dis - turb The Sound Of Si - lence.

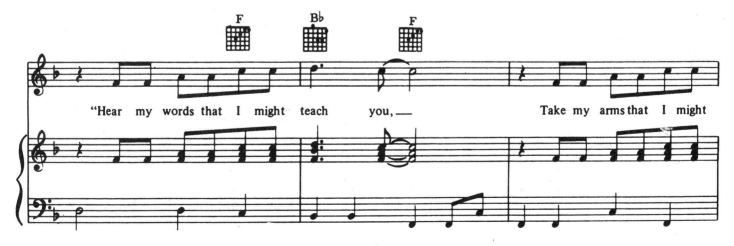

(4.) "Fools!" said I, "You do not know si - lence like a can - cer grows."

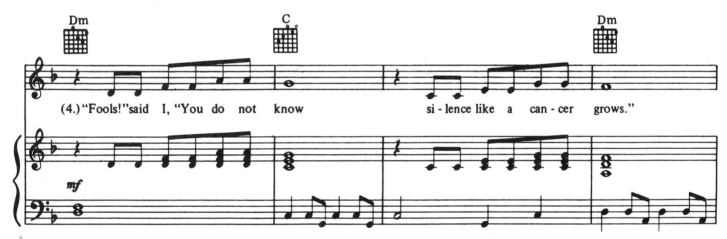

"Hear my words that I might teach you, Take my arms that I might

reach you." But my words like si - lent rain- drops

fell, and ech- oed _____ in the wells of

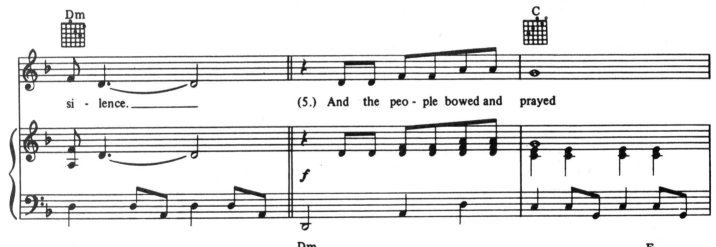

si - lence. _____ (5.) And the peo - ple bowed and prayed

to the ne - on god they made. And the sign flashed out its

127

Hearts And Bones

Words and Music by PAUL SIMON

One and one-half wan-der-ing Jews,___
back to__ the sea-son be-fore,___
One and one-half wan-der-ing Jews___

free to wan-der wher-ev-er__ they
look-ing back__ through the cracks in__ the
re-turned__ to their nat-u-ral

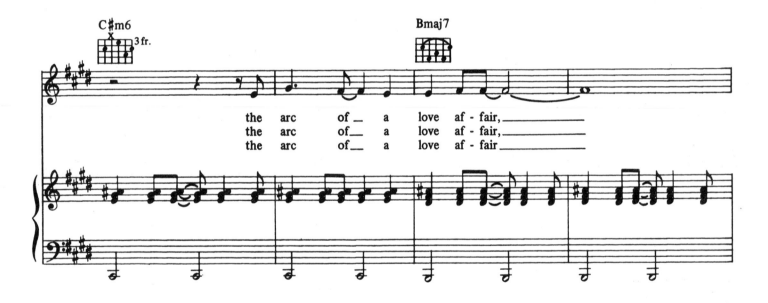

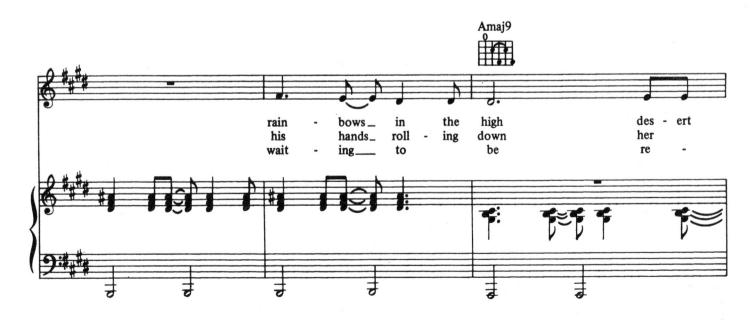

air.
hair.
stored.

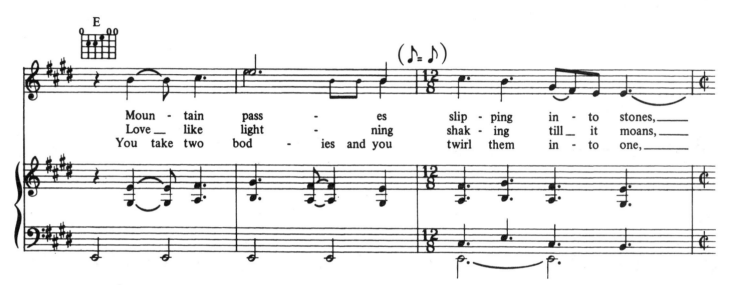

Moun - tain pass - - es slip - ping in - to stones,____
Love __ like light - ning shak - ing till __ it moans,____
You take two bod - ies and you twirl them in - to one,____

To Coda

hearts ___ and ___ bones, ____

hearts ___ and _____

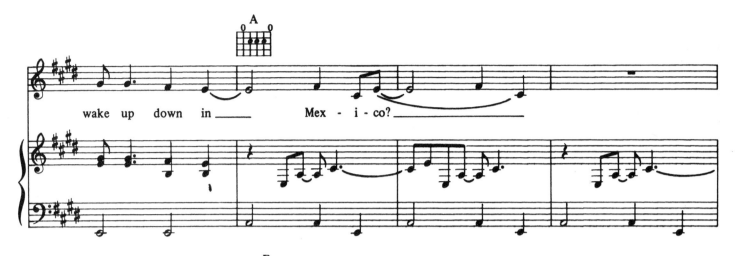

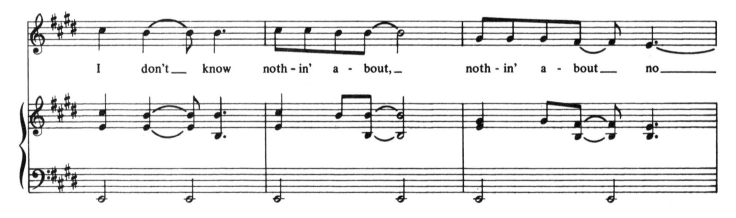

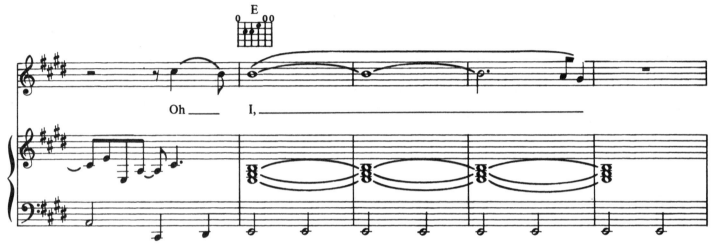

137

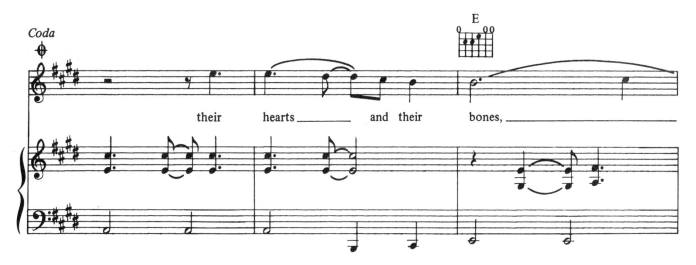

their hearts _____ and their bones, _____

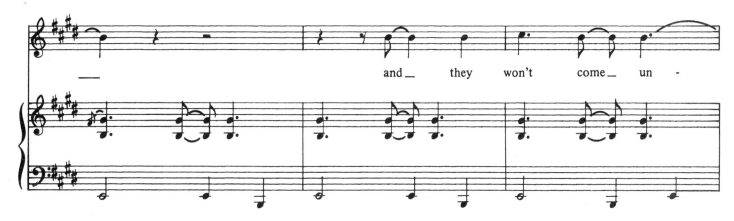

_____ and _ they won't come un -

done, _____ hearts_ and bones,_

hearts and bones,_

America

Words and Music by PAUL SIMON

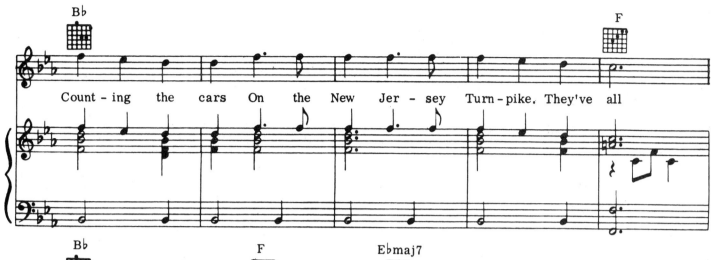

Count - ing the cars On the New Jer - sey Turn - pike. They've all

come _____ to look for A - mer _____ - i -

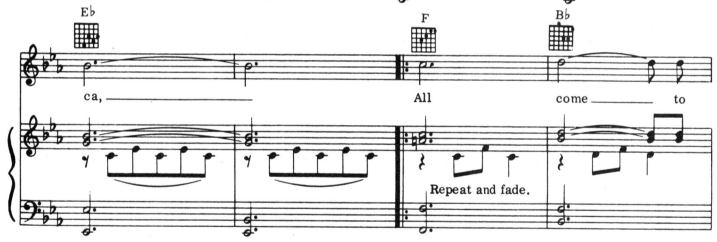

ca, _____ All come _____ to

Repeat and fade.

look for A - mer _____ - i - ca. _____

The Boxer

Words and Music by PAUL SIMON

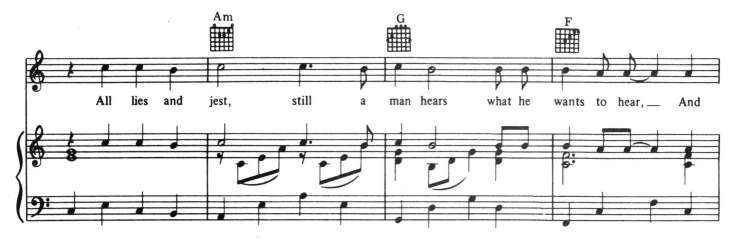

All lies and jest, still a man hears what he wants to hear, — And

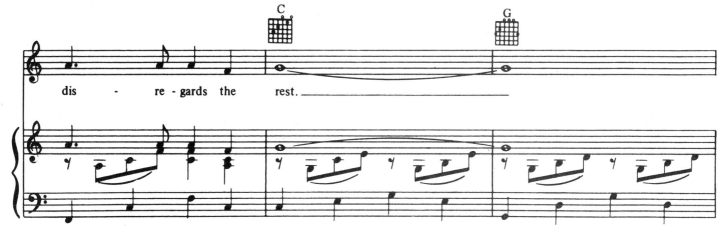

dis - re - gards the rest. _____

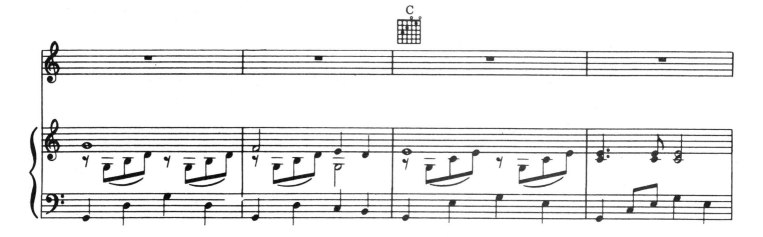

When I left my home and my fam - i - ly, — I was

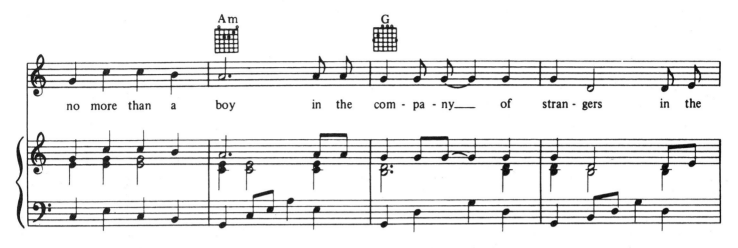

no more than a boy in the com - pa - ny___ of stran - gers in the

qui - et of a rail - way sta - tion run - ning scared, ___

Lay - ing low, seek - ing out the poor - er quar - ters where the

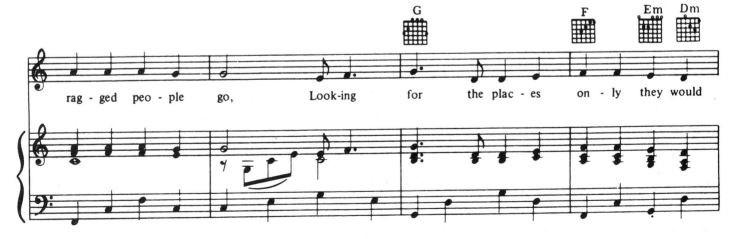

rag - ged peo - ple go, Look-ing for the plac - es on - ly they would

151

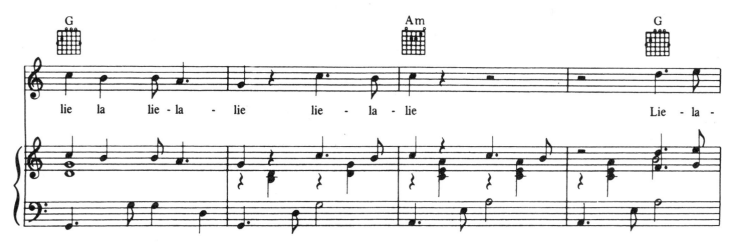

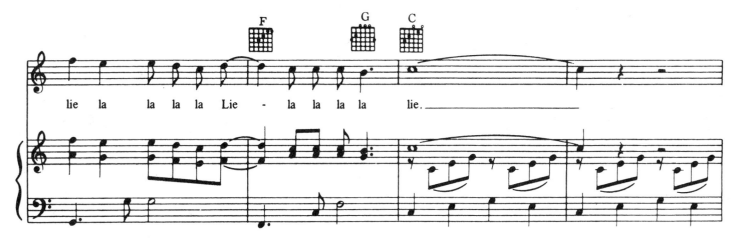

looking for a job, but I get no of - fers, _____ Just a

come-on from the whores_ on Sev-enth Av - e - nue._____

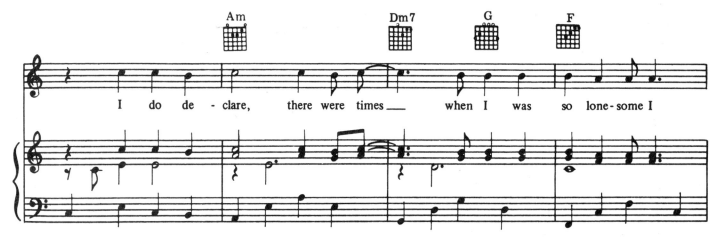

I do de - clare, there were times_ when I was so lone - some I

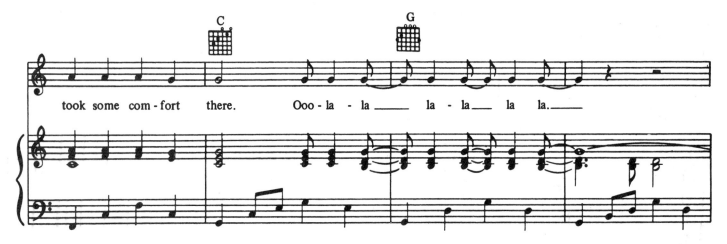

took some com - fort there. Ooo - la - la ___ la - la ___ la la.___

Then I'm lay - ing out my

win - ter clothes__ and wish - ing I was gone, ___ go - ing home

Where the New York Cit - y win - ters are - n't bleed - ing me, ___

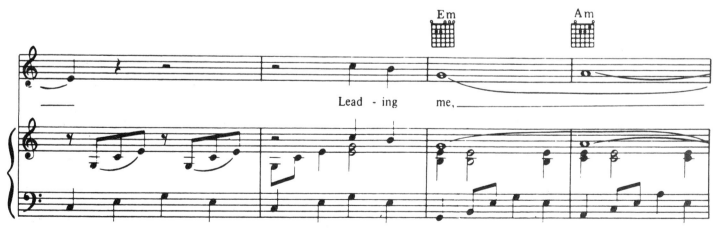

Lead - ing me, _____

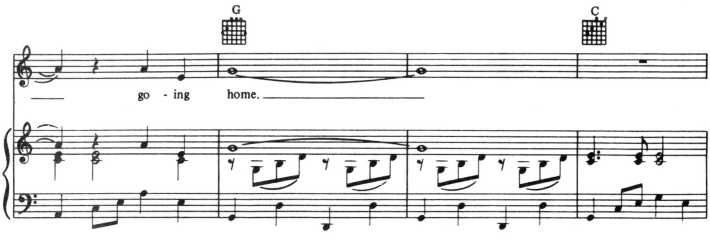

go - ing home.

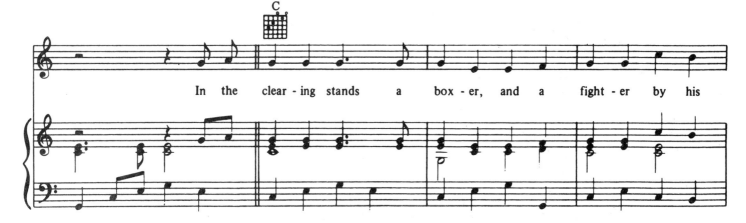

In the clear - ing stands a box - er, and a fight - er by his

trade, And he car - ries the re - mind - ers of ev - 'ry glove that

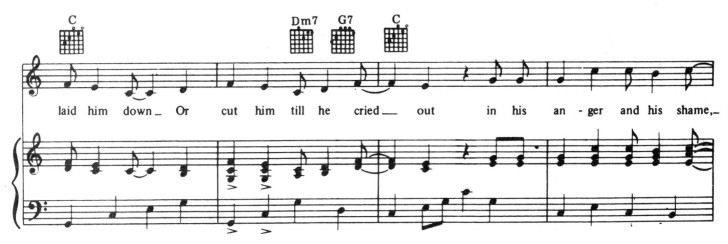

laid him down _ Or cut him till he cried _ out in his an - ger and his shame, _

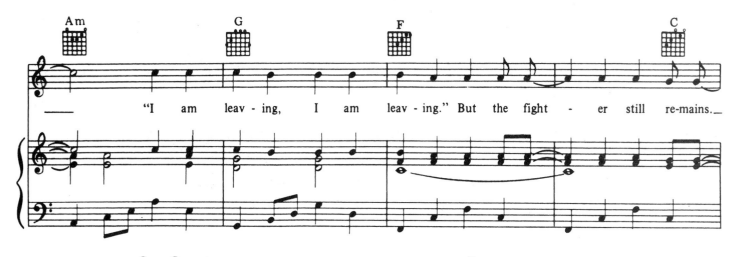

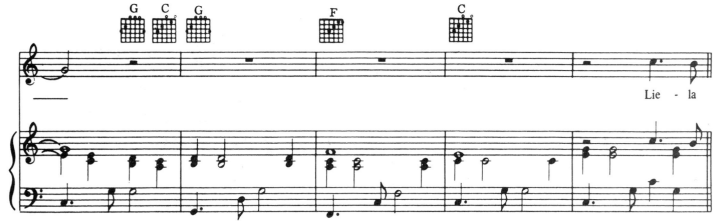

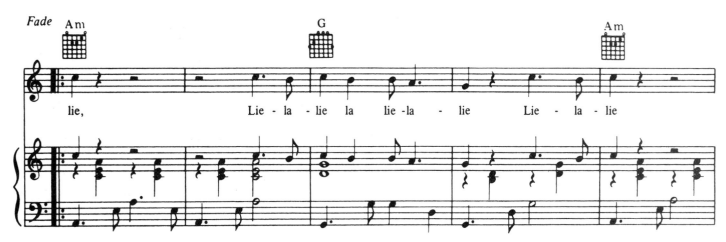

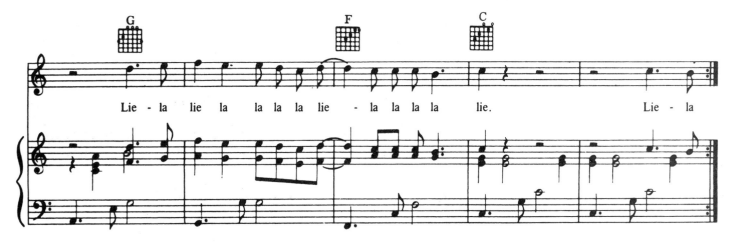

Cecilia

Words and Music by PAUL SIMON

Moderate, not too fast, rhythmically

Cel - ia, you're break-ing my heart,_ You're shak-ing my con - fi-dence dai -

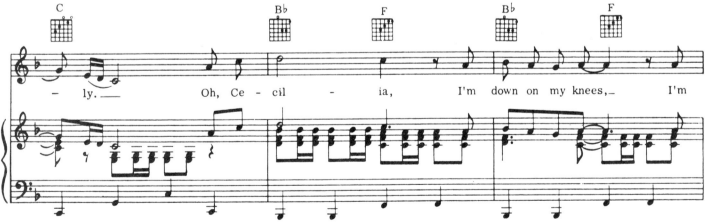

- ly. _ Oh, Ce - cil - ia, I'm down on my knees,_ I'm

157

beg-ging you please— to come home.— Ho - ho - home.—

— Mak-ing love— in the af - ter - noon— with Ce - ci -

- lia, Up in my— bed - room,— (mak-ing love——) I got up— to wash—

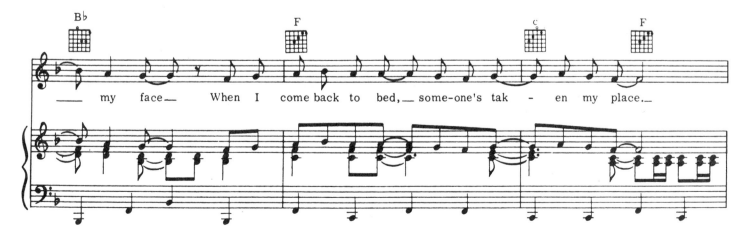

— my face— When I come back to bed,— some-one's tak - en my place.—

Cel - ia, You're break-ing my heart,__ You're shak-ing my con - fi - dence dai-

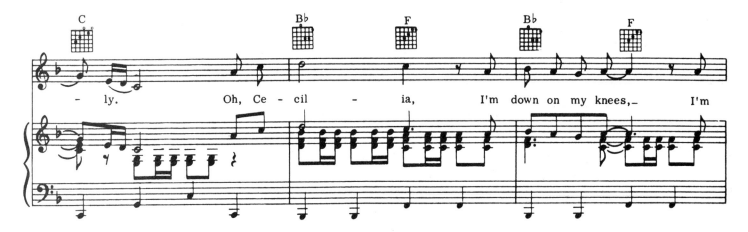

- ly. Oh, Ce - cil - ia, I'm down on my knees,__ I'm

beg-ging you please__ to come home.__ Come on home.__ Poh poh

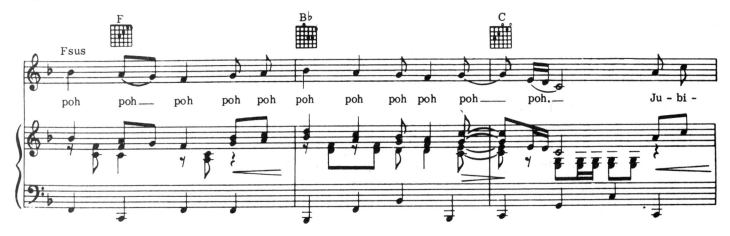

poh poh__ poh poh poh poh poh poh poh poh__ poh.__ Ju - bi -

la - tion, She loves me a - gain,___ I fall on the floor___ and I laugh-

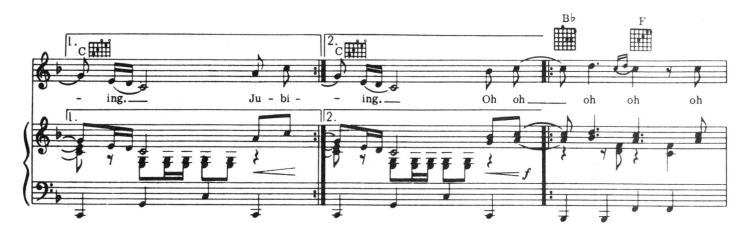

-ing.___ Ju - bi - -ing. Oh oh___ oh oh oh

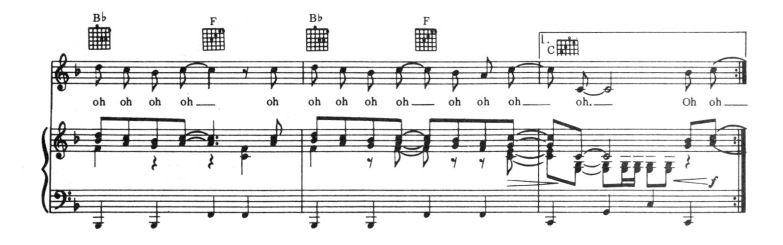

oh oh oh oh___ oh oh oh oh oh___ oh oh oh___ oh.___ Oh oh___

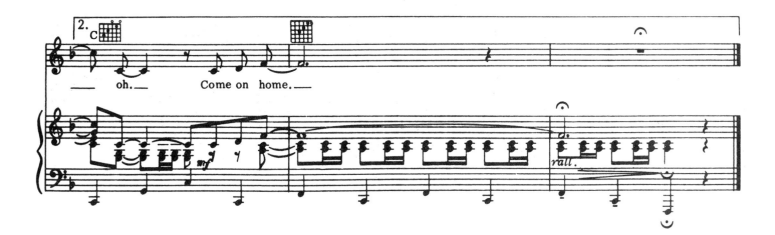

___ oh.___ Come on home.___

Late In The Evening

Words and Music by PAUL SIMON

The first thing I___ re-mem - ber, I___ was ly - ing in___ my bed.___
next thing I___ re-mem - ber, I___ am walk - in' down___ the street.___
learned to play___ some lead___ gui - tar.___ I was un - der-age___ in this

— I'm feel- in' all right. I'm with my boys. I'm with my troops,—
fun - ky bar. And I stepped out - side to smoke my - self a "J."—

I could-n't of been no more__ than one or two.

— yeah.—

I re-
And
And

mem - ber there's__ a ra - di - o__ com - in' from__ the room__
down a - long__ the av - e - nue,__ some guys were shoot - in' pool,__
when I came__ back to__ the room,__ ev - 'ry - bod - y just

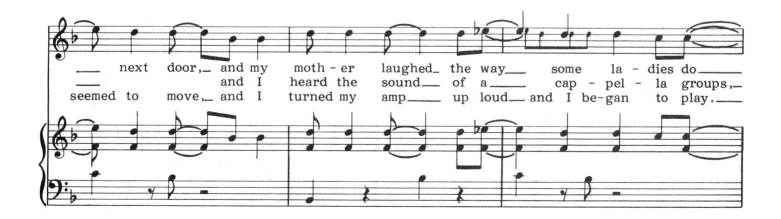

— next door,__ and my moth - er laughed__ the way__ some la - dies do__
and I heard the sound__ of a__ cap - pel - la groups,__
seemed to move,__ and I turned my amp__ up loud__ and I be-gan to play.__

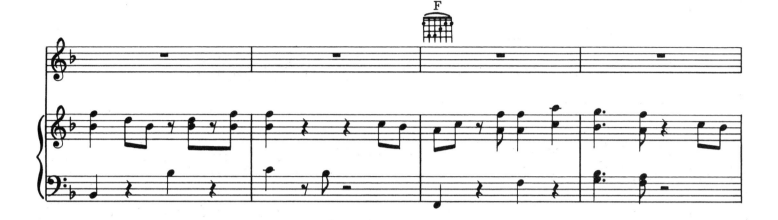

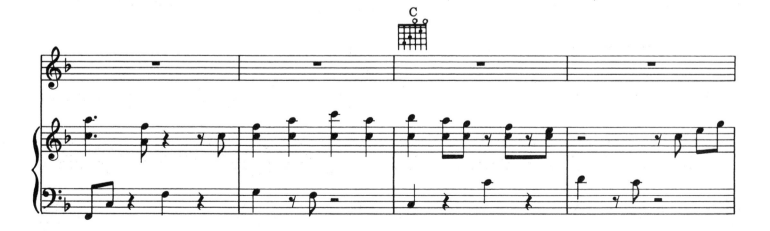

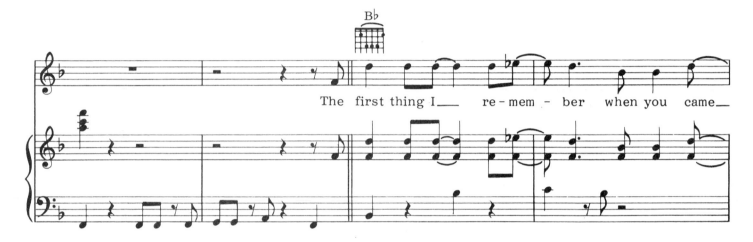

The first thing I__ re-mem-ber when you came__

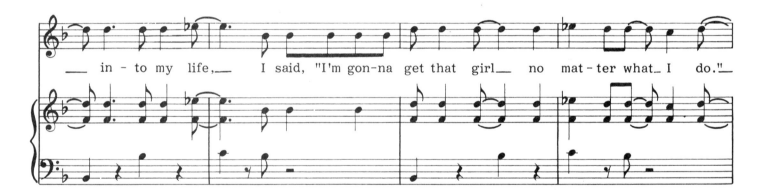

__ in-to my life,__ I said, "I'm gon-na get that girl__ no mat-ter what__ I do."__

Well, I

guess I'd been in love__ be-fore,__ and once or twice__ I been on__ the floor,__ but I

nev-er loved no one__ the way__ that I _____ loved you._____

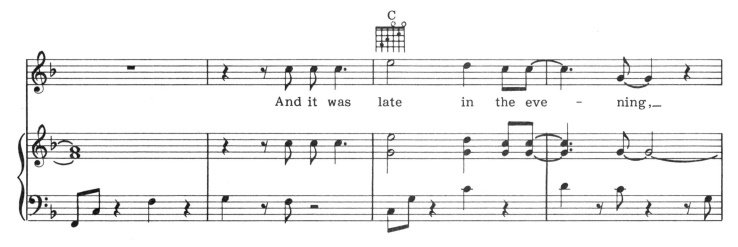

And it was late in the eve - ning,__

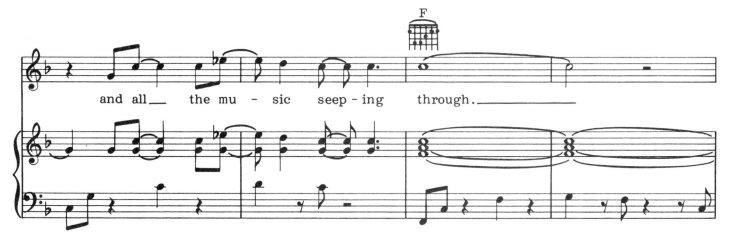

and all__ the mu - sic seep-ing through._____

D.S. % *al Coda* ⊕   Coda ⊕

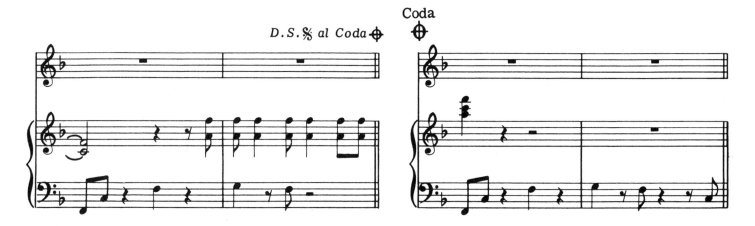

Repeat and fade

On August 15, 1991, Paul Simon brought his *Born At The Right Time* tour to New York's Central Park for a free concert on the Great Lawn. A crowd of 750,000 gathered to hear a retrospective mix of songs from the twelve-time Grammy winner's career, featuring favorites from the *Graceland* and *The Rhythm Of The Saints* albums along with classics such as "The Sound Of Silence," "Bridge Over Troubled Water" and "Still Crazy After All These Years." The 17-piece band—assembled from 3 continents—was joined by 10 drummers from the Bahian drum ensemble Grupo Cultural OLODUM to make an exhilarating musical and cultural event.

The Obvious Child

The Boy In The Bubble

She Moves On

Kodachrome®

Born At The Right Time

Train In The Distance

Me And Julio Down By The School Yard

I Know What I Know

The Cool, Cool River

Bridge Over Troubled Water

Proof

The Coast

Graceland

You Can Call Me Al

Still Crazy After All These Years

Loves Me Like A Rock

Diamonds On The Soles Of Her Shoes

Hearts And Bones

Late In The Evening

America

The Boxer

Cecilia

The Sound Of Silence

Amsco Publications
$24.95 in USA
Order No. PS 11261
US ISBN 0.8256.1337.X
UK ISBN 0.7119.2932.7

UPC

7 52187 11261 7